HUMAN BEHAVIOUR:

A Fascinating Look at Emotions, Superstitions and Body Language.

BY CRAIG JAMES BAXTER

2013

© 2013 by Craig James Baxter

All rights reserved. No part of this publication may be reproduced in any form or by any means, including scanning, photocopying or otherwise without prior written permission of the copyright holder.

First printing, 2013

Acknowledgements

This book could not have been written without the tireless research of many pioneering non-verbal experts who have not only inspired my interest in this fascinating profession, but have also generously donated their time to help me develop my understanding of human behaviour, emotions and non-verbal communication. Special thanks go (in no particular order) to: Dr. Desmond Morris, Dr. Paul Ekman, Prof. Aldert Vrij, Dr. David Givens, Prof. Steven Pinker and Mr. Joe Navarro, whose exceptional research in this field is nothing short of remarkable.

I would further like to acknowledge and extend my heart-felt gratitude to my fans on my website, my Facebook page (Understanding Body Language: Liars, Cheats and Happy Feet) and my Twitter page (@bodylanguageuk) for their fantastic support and valuable input whilst I was conducting research for this book.

I would also like to thank my good friend and business partner David Webb and his family for giving me the opportunity to showcase my passion on www.all-about-body-language.com and for his endless support and guidance.

My sister Samantha Baxter has given up a lot of her time to help me to structure and edit this book accurately, so she is also due a big thank you.

Finally, as I mentioned at the start of my previous two books, I would like to again thank my beautiful partner, Kat Whitley, as without her continued love and support, these books would have been a lot harder to write. Thank you also for keeping our two hyperactive Bengal kittens Willow and India distracted long enough for me to complete this book! After writing *Behind The Mask*, I promised that I would take her to New York (a fact which she reminds me of daily!) and I will eventually fulfil this promise. This is only my 3rd book, however I'm learning with each new edition how to balance my home and work life.

Dedication

I dedicate this book to the memory of my Uncle Colin who sadly passed away during the writing of this book.

Synopsis

As the author of the Amazon international #1 best-selling books 'Behind The Mask: What Michael Jackson's Body Language Told The World' and 'Unmasked: A Revealing Look At The Fascinating World Of Body Language' I felt that there was sufficient interest for me to expand a little more upon the intriguing world of human behaviour. Naturally, I have covered the study of human body language in both aforementioned books, however human interaction and behaviour is so much more than just reading body language. Granted that body language does play an integral role in everyday life (hence why it has earned a section in this book), however there are two other intriguing areas that I look forward to educating you about – emotions and superstitions.

In the opening section, I will guide you through the fascinating world of emotions so that you can become more adept at recognising emotions not only in yourself, but also in other people. I firmly believe that the vast majority of people have the capacity to recognise emotions in others and the information contained within this section will enable you to learn more.

In the second section, I take a look at some long-standing and some more modern superstitious beliefs which play a role in everyday life and highlight their often surprising origins. I had originally planned to focus this book entirely on emotions from the start, however after conducting research into emotions and their effect on everyday behaviour, I found that one area which frequently triggered the emotion of fear was breaking a believed superstition. I started this book in April 2013 and as I have now reached its climax in November 2013, it is abundantly clear that the fear some people face when not performing a superstition is truly fascinating and is more than worthy of a section in my book. I believe you will find it remarkable when I explain the degree to which certain sports stars have to perform superstitious ritualistic actions before a game or match in order to supposedly guarantee their victory. In this section, I also look at the full moon and the Ouija board to uncover how each has an effect on human behaviour, and additionally I will outline how some precious and semi-precious stones are believed to offer protection from various ills.

In the third section, I look at the importance of human body language in everyday life and I also underpin the importance of synchronisation between a person's words and their gestures when deciding upon the validity of their statement. For those who haven't read any of my previous work on non-verbal communication, I offer in this section an underpinning on how to use body language to your advantage in daily life, such as how to make a good confident first impression.

Finally, at the end of the book in Appendix 1, I give an account of two extreme emotional experiences (a skydive and hot air balloon flight) which I have successfully negotiated in order for the reader to understand that certain emotions such as fear can be overcome successfully. Contained within Appendix 2 is a guide to body language terminology to help you to further improve your knowledge of certain key terms.

By the time you reach the end of this book, I hope you will be one step closer to achieving your goal of learning more about emotions, superstitions and body language. This is by no means a comprehensive guide to these three areas, but rather it is intended as a short introduction to the topics. I felt it would be more beneficial to condense the key information down rather than overwhelm the reader with an overly- long and hard-to-access guide. You will find a list of further reading in the bibliography if you wish to research any of the topics covered in more depth.

After reading this book, you will discover that our behaviour is remarkably similar in one instance (genetic makeup, physiological changes, emotional responses, universal facial expressions) however incredibly varied on a cultural level. Superstitions for instance can be extremely cultural, and perhaps after reading this book, on your next foreign holiday you will be more interested in the beliefs, charms and amulets that signify a superstition in your chosen destination.

About the author

Craig 'CJB' Baxter has been studying emotions, body language and non-verbal communication for 10 years. Originally working in the medical profession, Craig's job is to support, help and give advice to patients in their quest for emotional and physical wellbeing. Craig has adapted his skills into observing human behaviour and relationships and then analysing the behaviour and body language on display. His background is in anatomy and physiology, and he has an in-depth knowledge of the human body and its movements.

Craig's debut book *'Behind The Mask: What Michael Jackson's Body Language Told The World'* became an Amazon international #1 bestseller in the Michael Jackson category (amongst others) in an astonishing 10 countries. Craig's book attracted high praise from both the Michael Jackson community and the eminent non-verbal experts whose research Craig cites in the book. Craig was interviewed by global news channel NTN 24 in August 2013 about the book's international success.

Craig's second book *'Unmasked: A Revealing Look At The Fascinating World Of Body Language'* achieved the much-converted #1 spot in the 'Behavioural Theory' category on Amazon in May 2013.

Since 2011, Craig's *Understanding Body Language: Liars, Cheats and Happy Feet* Facebook page has reached 45+ countries, and he has had his work translated into 11 languages. Currently, the page has over 5,830 followers. Craig is a master trainer in reading micro-expressions based on the training given by the Humintell company, making him the first in the United Kingdom to achieve this accolade. Craig has also completed a course in detecting deception using narrative analysis techniques (Statement Analysis®) with former federal law enforcement officer Mark McClish.

Furthermore, Craig is one of the most viewed body language decoders in YouTube's history, having amassed over 1,330,000 views and compiled over 120 body language analysis videos featuring celebrities, politicians, musicians and high profile criminal investigations.

Craig's All About Body Language website (www.all-about-body-language.com_) is part of a portfolio of psychology/forensic psychology/forensic science websites which together receive over 120,000 unique monthly visitors and generate over 4 million yearly page views.

Craig has written for numerous magazines and newspapers, composing articles on flirting, dating, interview techniques and lying and deception. Furthermore, Craig is a regular addition on national radio shows such as Radio Salford, educating listeners on how to spot flirting signs and improve their confidence (for instance at interviews) by altering their body language. Craig has also interviewed 25 of the world's leading body language experts such as Dr. Desmond Morris, Dr. Paul Ekman, Mr. Joe Navarro, Dr. David Matsumoto, Dr. Carol Kinsey Goman and J.J. Newberry, and if you are interested in reading the transcripts of these interviews, they can be accessed here: http://www.all-about-body-language.com/body-language-experts.html

CONTENTS PAGE

Synopsis 5
About the author 8
Introduction 12
Chapter 1: Emotions 16
    Emotions of humility, happiness and anger 26
    Happiness 27
    Anger 29
    Unsettling examples of happiness 30
Chapter 2: Superstitions 35
    Research into superstitions 35
    Superstitious rhymes, sayings and beliefs and their origins 39
    Charms and Amulets 49
    St. Christopher 51
    Peacock feathers 52
    Full moon 52
    The Ouija Board 54
    Modern internet-based superstitions Superstitions research 56
    Stones and superstitions 61
    Sports stars and superstitions 62
    Restaurant superstitions 69
    Lucky cat 72
    Aircraft superstitions 74
Chapter 3: Human body language 76
    Introduction 76
    Correctly reading facial emotions and identifying concealment. 77
    Timing and synchronisation of gestures and facial expressions. 81
    5 Essential Body Language Terms 84
    The Power of Body Language 87
    Body language and game playing 89
    Body language of a liar 90

Body language gestures and their meanings 94
Final thoughts 98
Appendix 1: Adrenaline-fuelled emotions 103
Appendix 2 : Body Language Terminology 112
Websites for further reading 120
Connect With Me 122

Introduction

Before I commence this book, I would like to take this opportunity to make an amendment from my second book *'Unmasked: A Revealing Look At The Fascinating World Of Body Language'*. In that book, I had taken a quite critical look at how I believed society will end up in the future, but perhaps I was being somewhat unfair in my predictions that the human race might one day turn into a dormant, reclusive species. After all, it was our primitive forebears' initial curiosity that shaped evolution as we know it. According to those who subscribe to the Darwinian theory of evolution, the tree-dwelling monkeys had to suppress their natural emotional instincts (such as to run and hide up a tree at the first sign of danger) in order to become the first hunter/gatherers and provide for their growing families. As eminent zoologist Dr Desmond Morris describes, *"This switch demanded a new mental attitude. There had to be an increase in co-operation, communication, intelligence, courage and the ability to concentrate for long periods of time on a specific goal"* (2006: 13). That inborn curiosity to hunt, farm and build has never left us, even if technology has made daily life easier than it was on the dry, dusty plains. Our tenacity as a species has all the hallmarks of making society work in the future, regardless of the somewhat alarming rapidity of technological advancements.

Interestingly, Channel 4 recently aired a fictional TV drama called *'Blackout'* which portrayed a total power failure in a major city for a week. It showed how life can quickly transform into anarchy when power is lost. People were invading the homes of others in search of food, water and portable generators, and the entire scenario in my opinion isn't that far away from reality, because our modern lives make huge demands upon our sources of energy and this is only going to increase as the population size booms. We have become so accustomed to our 24 hours a day lifestyle where we can go shopping or order fast food at any time of the day or night that we have forgotten what life was like before this was the norm. This show offered an insight into what life could be like if the script became a reality. Following on from this, there was a recent article on the BBC News website speculating about the extinction of our species that made an interesting point, namely that more academic papers each year are written about snowboarding than human extinction. Despite these fears and some people's doom-mongering that a pandemic or a natural disaster may wipe us all off the face of the earth, the article does offer some reassuring advice, *'because as a species we've already outlasted many thousands of years of disease, famine, flood, predators, persecution, earthquakes and environmental change. So the odds remain in our favour'.* Dr. Bostrom (the director of the institute which conducted the research) believes we've entered a new kind of technological era with the capacity to threaten our future as never before, and he mentions the rise of Artificial Intelligence and synthetic biology (where biology meets engineering). These are "*threats we have no track record of surviving*" - he likened them to a dangerous weapon in the hands of a child and said that the advances in technology have overtaken our capacity to control the possible consequences.

The trouble is, like I mentioned in *'Unmasked'*, is that our developed brains are never at rest; we are constantly finding new advancements in technology. Sadly, these advancements usually come at a price - a price paid by unskilled manual workers whose duties have been replaced by emotionless machines. From a business viewpoint, deciding to invest in machines to replace the human touch might result in higher profits on a spreadsheet, but the reality is that those whose jobs have now been replaced are thrown back into the vastly competitive employment pool. I read a shocking statistic recently, that 26% of the Spanish population is currently unemployed, which equates to a staggering 5 million people (Daily Mail 2013). Therefore there has never been a better time to learn more about the importance of emotions and body language to help bolster your confidence to help you find work or become more successful in your life in general. If you do find yourself currently out of work, then I urge you to read the section named 'How To Impress During A Job Interview' in my second book *Unmasked*, as the advice will certainly increase your chances of gaining employment.

You might think that the topics I cover in this book are quite random, however all three chapters have strong and interconnected links with each other. Emotions are registered in the body and reveal themselves through a variety of channels, most prominently through autonomic physiological changes (whitening/flushing of the face, pupil dilation/constriction, sweating, micro-expressions of emotion) but also through our conscious and unconscious body language. Superstitious beliefs play on our mind and emotions, with the emotion of 'fear' often playing the lead role in the chosen belief. The fear is about what punishment will occur for not following through with a superstition or because a ritualistic superstitious action has been forgotten or not carried out in its entirety (this is particularly prevalent with certain sports stars – see chapter two). Some superstitions such as breaking a mirror come with a very specific punishment (7 years' bad luck) whereas for others such as walking under a ladder or failing to salute a magpie you are just risking bringing general bad luck upon yourself – if you are a believer of course! Some superstitions are as old as the hills, such as not opening an umbrella indoors or not putting new shoes on the table, and the origin of these beliefs are often varied and surprising. However, with the rise of social media, texting and emailing, some new superstitions have made their way into prominence and I will cover these in chapter two.

Certain sports stars have very specific superstitious beliefs, such as tennis star Rafael Nadal, golfer Tiger Woods and many others whose actions are covered later on in the book. Body language has a role in identifying emotions, however it also plays a fascinating role within superstitious beliefs too, such as crossing oneself or one's fingers, saluting a magpie, touching wood, rubbing a lucky charm etc. Each topic I cover is as fascinating as the last, and I do hope that by the time you reach the end of this book, you will have at your fingertips information to further increase your own knowledge. Maybe you will even be able to educate others should any of the topics I cover be brought up in conversation.

I do hope that you will find the following three chapters interesting, engaging and informative, and they should provide you with a better understanding of the modern (and sometimes unbelievable) world we live in. Again, this is by no means a comprehensive look at emotions, superstitions and body language, but merely a taster of these three fascinating elements in the world around you. The book as a whole should assist you in further understanding the behaviour of others.

Chapter 1: Emotions

Quite simply, emotions play an integral role in everyday life and are unconscious reactions to events that are important to our wellbeing. They can be triggered by incidents as varied as hearing the news that a loved one has disappeared, finding a £50 note on the floor or discovering you have been made redundant with immediate effect. All three plausible scenarios would be sufficient to trigger an emotional response in the body which would reveal itself in a variety of changes in behaviour. Also, breaking a believed superstition would in some people trigger a range of emotions which will be discussed in more detail in chapter two.

What is an emotion?

There have been many attempts to answer this question which have often been provided by psychologists, however I feel the best answer is to state that emotions are a complex state of feelings that result in a variety of physical and physiological changes which influence thought and behaviour. Such changes enable the person to deal with the trigger (the situation) effectively and without thought. As leading emotions expert Dr. Paul Ekman states in his book *'Emotional Revealed'* *"Emotions also send out signals: changes in our expressions, face, voice and bodily posture. We don't choose these changes; they simply happen"* (2003: 3).

I had intended to write a book about emotions and human behaviour much further on in my non-verbal career, however the trigger and the catalyst for writing this book came as I was sat writing an article for my local paper about the importance of body language in a job interview. As I was deep in concentration, my 9 month old Bengal kitten India leapt up at me unexpectedly, sending me into an unconscious, immediate retreat. My heart rate instantly elevated and I instinctively retreated back in my chair and used my flailing arms to shield myself from this sudden impending impact. This reaction was triggered instantaneously but in the subsequent seconds that passed (after realising it was only India and nothing untoward) I felt my heart rate slowly decrease and return to normal. After giving India some fuss, I resumed the article on body language, and it was then when I had that *Eureka!* moment. My experience reminded me of an experiment that I had read about conducted by Charles Darwin in 1872 where he had observed a puff adder behind glass in a zoo. He stayed as close to the glass for as long as he could, trying to over-ride his sense of fear. However, in the end, when the snake struck the glass in an attempt to bite, Darwin instinctively jumped backwards. He could not, no matter how hard he tried, over-ride his body's instinctive and inbuilt reaction to something coming towards it quickly and unexpectedly. His discovery 141 years ago still rings true today, namely that instantaneous reactions such as the ones we both experienced are hardwired into our brains, and for a very good reason – our own preservation. Darwin's exact account of this experiment was published in his pioneering book *The Expressions of the Emotions of Man and Animals*' – "*I put my face to the thick glass-plate in front of a puff adder in the Zoological Gardens with the firm determination of not starting back if the snake struck at me; but as soon as the blow was struck, my resolution went for nothing, and I jumped a yard or two backward with astonishing rapidity. My will and reason were powerless against the imagination of a danger which had never been experienced*" (1872). This example shows that emotions provide us with split-second reactions that are governed by our subconscious. They are performed immediately and without conscious thought. If my brain had to consciously decide if India was friend or foe, this could have been fatal due to the time it would have taken to decide. Instead, your brain automatically protects you from the unexpected invasion and performs the necessary defence.

"When we are in the grip of an emotion, a cascade of changes occurs in split seconds without our choice or immediate awareness, in: the emotional signals in the face and voice; preset actions; learned actions; the autonomic nervous system activity that regulates our body; the regulatory patterns that continuously modify our behaviour; the retrieval of relevant memories and expectations; and how we interpret what is happening within us and in the world. These changes are involuntary; we don't choose them" (Ekman 2003:82)

Another example of a split-second emotional reaction happened as I was enjoying a meal in a local Indian restaurant for my mother's birthday. A balloon suddenly popped behind my chair, forcing me to duck down and cover my head (almost getting a face full of Lamb Madras in the process - much to the amusement of friends and family!) Afterwards, I informed them that the reaction was part of my emotional alert database. The sudden noise alerted my emotional centre in my brain, and as it couldn't see what made the noise (or verify its seriousness) my brain sent an immediate message which made me duck and cover my head which is the most valuable area, as my back was protected by the chair. Your emotions don't care about whether you make a fool of yourself in public, as their job is to keep you safe. This action was an instinctive in-built reaction that we all have hard-wired within us. I was capable of reacting quickly because I am a physically conditioned man, so my reaction time was helped by my fast-twitch muscle actions, which enabled me to react that millisecond quicker than someone not as conditioned. This is another example of how fear can trigger immediate reactions in the body designed to keep you alive as long as possible and protect you from perceived dangers. Protection is hard wired into our primitive brain, however a great number of people take the notion of protection to another level with the belief that some personal adornments have the power to fend off evil spirits and protect them from bad luck or misfortune. I will cover these in more detail later on in chapter 2.

As I have addressed above, think of your emotions as being similar to the pre-programmed anti-virus software on your computer – it is always running silently in the background scanning for any threat to its working system, and its reaction to danger is instantaneous. As such, your emotions have the ability to, at times, override your conscious decision-making. Upon the detection of a threat, our emotions will subconsciously change the internal mechanisms in the body to act accordingly and remedy the perceived threat. Interestingly, the danger doesn't need to have happened yet, as the sensation could be a remembered thought where a significant moment was re-experienced and the emotion comes flooding back. Sometimes the intensity of the emotion won't be as strong as that felt at the time of the actual event - it might only be a fragment of what you originally experienced. Occasionally, when we reminisce about a highly emotional situation, we won't experience the same emotion we felt at the time, but another entirely different one. Fear for instance is an example, especially if there was no reason to be afraid in the first place, as you might look back on reflection and think "why was I scared?", particularly if you were frightened of something that transpired not to be a threat at all. For instance, you may feel contempt towards the person who played the trick on you which caused you to embarrass yourself through fright, or happiness towards the person who organised a surprise birthday party for you which originally frightened you when everybody jumped out from behind the furniture. Dr. Ekman makes a valid point when he states that *"Memories about emotional events, those that we choose to call to mind, which do not immediately cause us to re-experience the original felt emotions, provide an opportunity to learn how to re-construe what is happening in our life so that we have a chance to change what is making us emotional"* (2003: 50).

Whilst on the subject of recalled emotions, during the mid 1930s, Russian film director Constantin Stanislavski coined what is known as the 'Stanislavski Acting Technique'. This is used to teach an actor how to accurately portray certain key emotions to the audience by learning how to remember and re-experience heightened emotions that they have previously encountered. If the actor is unable to feign the required emotion in a convincing way during their performance, they are taught to remember an actual experience that would trigger the necessary emotion. For instance, recalling a pet dying, the smell of rotting food or the feeling of road rage would fill the body with the required negative emotion. This will result in the reliable facial muscles being contracted and the all-important correct body language being shown to avoid others suspecting that this emotional display is not genuine. Remember that certain emotions are unconscious reactions to matters that are deeply important to our wellbeing, however when we consciously trigger an emotion it can deceive the onlooker into believing it to be genuine.

Emotional recognition and the face

Emotional recognition is evolving rapidly with advancements in technology, as for instance, facial recognition software is at the cutting edge of science. A specific example of this can be found on the Humintell (emotional recognition training) website, which describes a coffee machine which was installed at an airport in South Africa, and remarkably it had been designed not to accept money, but only to dispense coffee when it recognised a tired look on people's faces. At first, this left many people puzzled, but the machine was programmed to only dispense coffee when it recognised a yawn on people's faces. This goes to show that facial recognition technology is developing at an astonishing rate and may have many varied applications in the future. The reason this machine worked was because the yawn is a universal facial expression linked to tiredness, fatigue and boredom.

In my second book *'Unmasked'* I added that *"One aspect people fail to recognise is that some people often conceal their sadness until they are with those who can provide comfort and support"* (Baxter, 2013: 17). The face is a good transmitter of this attempted concealment of sadness, as someone may press their lips together in an attempt to distort the facial message being sent to onlookers. This is performed because not everyone feels the suffering of others. *"Some people become angry in response to another person's misery. They may feel that an unwelcome, improper demand is being made upon them for help"* (Ekman, 2003:108). This is a possible reason why some people find it difficult to open up if they are not in the presence of someone they trust not to become frustrated at their grief. How often have you said to yourself 'he/she doesn't *look* that upset'. This could be because that person is managing their true feelings until they are with those who will support their sadness. Once they are with that person who can provide comfort, they will reveal their emotions without the fear of ill-feeling. Quite humorously, I experienced this very scenario when watching the climatic ending to the Premier League football final in 2012. As a devout Manchester United fan, the agony I experienced when rival club Manchester City scored the winner in injury time was so strong that I remained silent for hours after the game had finished. I watched the game at home with my partner Kat, who can't abide football. She did not share the sadness I felt, and instead she reminded me that 'it's only a game' and suggested that I should 'grow up!' Because she was unable to provide the support I needed, I concealed my anguish until I found the much-needed solace of a fellow Manchester United fan hours later. If you are interested in watching my priceless reaction to the moment Sergio Aguero scored the winner then you can watch it on my YouTube channel (search for CJBAXXTER).

There are certain pitfalls when it comes to reading the face. Attempted behavioural control enables us to consciously contract most of our facial muscles to create many facial expressions - expressions that we don't necessarily feel (as seen in the above example of the actor). Skilled poker players are great at both masking and falsifying expressions to bluff their opponents into believing they have either a good or a bad hand. As Dr. Morris states *"Nowhere is the suppression of body language more important, however, than in the sphere of professional poker. In this essentially simple card game, large sums of money are won and lost according to the bluffing ability of the individual players. A player who can conceal his pleasure at a good hand or his disappointment at a bad one is able to turn his self-control into considerable profit"*. (1994:38)

Dr. Morris continues and makes another fascinating observation about the controlled facial expressions of emotion (or rather the lack of) seen during a 1993 poker tournament. *"The winner - from Arizona - was so completely deadpan throughout the competition that he found it difficult to return to ordinary body language. After four gruelling days of intense play, when he had finally won the million dollars, his face refused to show any emotion. Immediately after his moment of triumph, he stood up and walked to the centre of the room. There, still deadpan, he stabbed his right forefinger into the air in a symbolic coup de grace. As he turned away, his face remained expressionless. Only when he moved across to the side of the arena and was embraced by his excited wife and daughter did he, at long last, allow himself a broad, triumphant smile"* (1994:41).

Instantaneous emotional reactions

As I have previously mentioned, emotions produce a variety of changes in the body and affect how we react to the world and those around us. The emotion of 'fear' for example will trigger an elevation of the sympathetic nervous system, resulting in: an increase in heart rate (more demand for oxygenated blood to be diverted to the arms and legs to run or fend off an attack), the widening of the eyes (more of the sclera or the whites of the eyes becomes visible), the dilation of the pupils (to allow better vision), the raising of the eyebrows and finally the stretching of the mouth. The emotion of fear sends a signal to the body that something is wrong and you need to pay attention, which is why our senses are elevated during fear. These changes happen without conscious thought or control. Our subconscious autonomic actions prevent our much slower conscious choices from taking over the situation and delaying our response time. In fear, the faster we can react, the faster we can defend ourselves against the danger. Dr. Ekman expands on the emotion of fear by stating that *"When we feel any type of fear, when we are conscious of being afraid, it is hard to feel anything else or think about anything else for a time. Our mind and our attention are focused on the threat. When there is an immediate threat, we focus until we have eliminated it, or if we find that we can't, our feelings may turn into terror. Anticipating the threat of harm can also monopolize our consciousness for long periods of time, or such feelings may be episodic, returning from time to time"* (2003: 174).

As I have previously mentioned, emotions are instantaneous and can be triggered in less than a second, and often the briefest way they reveal themselves is through various facial expressions. The hit US TV show '*Lie To Me*' sparked a more widespread interest in micro-expressions and brought their existence into popular culture. Micro-expressions are signs of concealed emotions which flash very quickly on the face when the necessary emotion is triggered – they are a reliable indicator that issues are present and **not** (contrary to popular thought) a sign that someone is necessarily lying. The problem, as I mentioned in *Unmasked*, is that micro-expressions happen so quickly that you are likely to miss them before you've had chance to recognise that it was indeed an emotion revealing itself facially. I myself used the training of Dr. David Matsumoto's company 'Humintell' to hone and sharpen my emotional recognition skills, as well as Dr. Ekman's extensive training tools. As Dr. Matsumoto describes, microexpressions occur *"so fast they happen in the blink of an eye – as fast as $1/15^{th}$ of a second. The reason that they happen so quick is that the individual is trying to conceal them"* (2011:6). So therefore, training yourself to become adept at spotting the muscle actions of the face which reveal emotions will help you to ascertain the mood and sentiments of your conversation partner.

Emotional variations

One aspect of emotions that I feel has been frequently misunderstood is their great variety. Granted that we do not all behave the same way in any given situation, however there are universal basic emotions, each of them with their own particular set of behavioural characteristics. These enable the trained observer to identify (with a certain degree of accuracy) whether or not the other person is genuinely experiencing what they are describing in a statement. Often it is the absence of emotion which can be more revealing rather than the presence of one, which makes things slightly easier for the lie-catcher because certain emotions can be falsified better than others. Skilled law enforcement officers are trained to detect the subtle and frequently missed signs of concealed emotions on the face. If you are interested in learning more about law enforcement techniques then I recommend reading Dr. David Matsumoto's 2011 FBI Law Enforcement Bulletin *'Evaluating Truthfulness and Detecting Deception: New Tools to Aid Investigators'*. The link to this article can be found in the bibliography section.

Chapter 1: Emotions

How we manage and express our behaviour can often be dictated by our locality. These are referred to as 'display rules' and act like social etiquettes. Sometimes we have reason to tone down our emotions, like in the example I gave in my second book *'Unmasked'* – *"A mother who has recently lost her child in tragic circumstances must, to a certain extent, hide her true feelings. If she were too successful in concealing her mourning, she would be criticised for a lack of feeling. Equally, if she failed to display some visible restraint of her grief, she would be said to lack courage and self-control. Her 'brave face' is therefore an example of pseudo-deception, where the deceiver is happy to be found out. Either consciously or unconsciously, she wants the forced smile that she uses to be read as forced"* (Baxter, 2013:16). In contrast, in other situations, it is totally acceptable to express our emotions outwardly by screaming, shouting and showing unreserved adulation. Depending on your personality, this could be upon hearing the news that you've just gained employment after years of job hunting, watching your favourite football team win the big cup after numerous attempts, or realising that you've won a substantial amount of money on the lottery. Either way, how we display our emotions is decided upon by many external factors, and despite our unconscious mind controlling the physiological response in the body, it's often left up to our conscious mind to decide what to do after the initial trigger has worn off.

People who manipulate our emotions can be found in every walk of life. I have an advantage because of my background in human behaviour and reading body language, so I can recognise some of the tactics used to manipulate me into taking a course of action that I might not otherwise have taken on my own. Car salesmen can use certain psychological tactics to influence you into buying a car that you don't need or want. My friend and eminent US psychologist Dr. Michael Britt wrote an excellent book about the topic called *"They Saw You Coming – Psychological Tactics Car Dealers Use to Get You*

To Buy" (2013). These tricks are not just exclusive to car salesmen though. There are those at work who will manipulate your emotions to get their own way - they will wear you down and strike. I have personally been on the receiving end of numerous attempts to coerce me into covering extra shifts against my wishes. Despite saying no, people will use a variety of tricks to attempt to change your mind, and Dr. Britt expands upon one such trick below.

"Here's an example. You mention that you want a safe car because you've got a family. So the dealer shows you a car with a good safety record, but it's more than you want to spend. You might hear this: "Well you did say that you wanted a safe car and you know, safety features sometimes do cost a little extra. I'm just trying to get you the car you want" (he's throwing in a little "aren't I a nice guy?"). Be aware that if you say enough about yourself during these "harmless" conversations you are just giving the dealer more information to pick and choose from to get you to be consistent with what you just said" (Britt, 2013:12).

Emotions of humility, happiness and anger

Humility

I will now describe an incident which reminds us of the importance of having a sense of humility toward strangers. As Kat and I were doing some shopping in Manchester on a busy Saturday afternoon in Winter, we had to walk past a group of homeless people who had huddled in a doorway for warmth. It was quite surreal to watch as not one person on the crowded street offered to help these poor dishevelled fellow beings. I felt compelled and gave one of the homeless men my hot drink. He didn't say a word to me as he accepted my drink, but his smile will live long in my memory. As I walked away, Kat gave me a kiss on the cheek, and what had just occurred between myself and the homeless man reminded me that despite our vast personality differences, we are all the same animal. Some may be bigger, some may be stronger, but we are all the same evolved animal. I believe that we are all capable of compassion but different things tug at the heart strings. I for instance can become quite overwhelmed with grief when I see an animal suffering, and there is one advert currently on British television that makes me feel a terrible sadness. It's an RSPCA advert where a cat is left meowing at its owner's window, unbeknownst that his master has sadly passed away. I, like many, feel the suffering of animals more than the suffering of fellow humans. I would hazard a guess that the homeless man who I helped would have received more money or food if he had a dog sat with him. There must be a psychological reason for this, one in which I will research in my future endeavours. Desmond Morris makes an excellent point about humility in his book *'The Nature of Happiness'* (2006) where he states that charity workers look upon strangers as an extension of their own family, meaning that they don't differentiate between their suffering and that of a loved one. I have shaved my head, run 10 mile road races and flung myself out of a perfectly functioning aeroplane (or a detailed description of my skydive experience, see appendix 2) to raise money for various charities and each experience gave me a real sense of giving something back. You never know when you will fall on hard times, so learning to give helps you to truly appreciate everything you have.

Happiness

"Happiness is not something ready made. It comes from your own actions" - Dalai Lama

Throughout our lives, we are in constant pursuit of happiness, and it's something which we all desire. However, the definition of happiness varies tremendously depending on your outlook. The homeless person I mentioned flashed me an expression of elated happiness when I offered him a drink, and Kat literally jumped for joy when she heard that her best friend was engaged. However, not all happiness is linked with positivity. What makes one person happy could be wasted on another. When Kat brings home yet another brand new pair of designer shoes, it fills me with the sensation of "Why?! You have hundreds of pairs!" She doesn't feel what I feel. To her, they are her prize for working hard and being able to afford the occasional luxury. Interestingly, I remember one occasion where she told me that she had been 'hunting' in the shops for months for this one particular handbag that she had seen online. I reminded her that her words were very reminiscent of what life was like before we evolved into homosapians. The fact that she 'hunted' for the handbag is very symbolic, as hunting is hardwired into our enlarged evolved brains. Alas, the vast majority of us no longer hunt animals for sustenance, but we replicate the act of hunting via a number of channels, such as 'hunting' for a bargain at the local designer store or waiting for the right time to 'strike' when the sales have been announced. Her new shoes are just a trivial reminder that we feel happiness about different things and our hunting actions have changed over time.

Dr. Morris further expands on this: "We not only use symbolic speech, but also make symbolic equations in every sphere of our activities. And we are so good at symbolizing that we can experience an intense happiness from a symbolic success, a happiness just as real as if we were engaged in the original, primeval model of which the symbolic act is a copy. To give a personal example, one of my great joys is going on a book-hunt. Finding a rare book I desperately want after a long search, acquiring it and carrying it home with me, is a symbolic equivalent of a primeval hunt for prey. Yes, I still need to hunt because I am human, but no, I do not have to kill a wild animal to satisfy my ancient biological hunting urge" (Morris, 2006: 20).

Some people deliberately attempt to falsify an emotion for personal gain or to see how successful they can be at this 'game', because if they do succeed, it will provide them with feelings of both happiness and self-satisfaction. Those who feign illness at the doctors for time off work fall into this category. Again, this is where body language comes into play. If the duper can successfully synchronise their words and movements so they fit succinctly together, then there is very little chance of their deception being discovered. I am not suggesting that we all play games such as this to provide us with a moment of delight (known in this case as Duper's delight), but unfortunately, there will always be those who will. Duper's delight is so-called because the duper feels happiness that his deception has been successful when the doctor believes his story that his back is sore, particularly if this allows him to spend a few days at home while his superiors perform an audit of his office so that he doesn't have to worry about being held responsible for any issues.

Anger

Anger can be a very destructive emotion. In anger transference, you transfer your original emotion that would get you into trouble away from the person who is the target of your rage and you instead transfer it to an innocent victim. In this classic example, the employee has had a deeply unpleasant interaction with his boss, so upon returning home, he takes his frustration out on his wife. His wife attempts to regain her own self-respect after suffering humiliation by snapping at their son, who then proceeds to take his anger out on the family cat (this is often known as 'kicking the cat').

It might seem ridiculously obvious, but one must remember not to become angry, frustrated or even physically aggressive when someone experiences happiness in something you don't find enjoyable. Kat makes the same characteristic facial expression each time I put the football on TV – a mixture of distain and boredom – and there is no need to be adept at spotting micro-expressions here! Darwin suggested that as evolved apes, we would have had to compromise during our evolutionary times, such as deciding who would stay at home and defend the territory and who would hunt for food. If our ancestors could learn the social skills necessary to co-operate with one another, then the least we can do is extend the same courtesy to our fellow beings. Sadly, respect for one another is something that society often lacks, and this was put into sharp focus recently when 3 teenage boys were jailed in Liverpool for beating a defenceless homeless man to death for a dare. The judge in the case said *'I think it is a desperately sad reflection on this society that each of you was party to serious violence purely for the sake of it.'* (BBC news website, April 13).

Unsettling examples of happiness

At the other end of the happiness spectrum are behaviours that seldom rank in everyday thought - those who find great pleasure in manipulating, hurting and destroying fellow human beings and animals. A very distressing example of this occurred as I was writing the opening sections of this book (in April 2013) when two terrorist bombs exploded at the Boston Marathon, killing three people including an 8 year old boy and critically injuring many others. I have previously criticised social media as I believe it could eventually cause the reading of body language to become a lost art. However, as all the mobile phone networks in Boston were shut

Chapter 1: Emotions

down in the immediate aftermath of the incident to prevent any more devices from being triggered remotely, social media played a crucial role in allowing people to communicate with loved ones to verify their safety. The media asked local business in Boston to unlock their Wi-Fi networks in order to allow people to access internet facilities on their phones so they could contact missing family members.

Despite the fact that the vast majority of the games people play are psychological, some people find great delight and happiness in inflicting physical pain on others. Here, the sadist subjects their victim to harm in order to satisfy his craving for absolute power. The victim accepts the beating as they often feel powerless to stop the continuous torment. Dominance is not just resigned to acts of physical torment. I have encountered many people who told me that their ex-partner was a control freak, when really all the person was doing was expressing their own thoughts and ideas which may not necessarily have been the same as theirs. Dale Carnegie states in his book *'How To Win Friends And Influence People'* (1981) that everyone has a desire to feel important. One area he did not mention is that sadly, some people go to extreme measures to feel important, even if that means destroying other people in the process.

Quite worryingly, another aspect of happiness that most people don't consider is the rise of the suicide bomber. The thought of savagely killing innocent people fills the terrorist with an almost euphoric sensation (one which he must conceal to avoid detection). This is because he has been brainwashed into believing that his sacrifice will be duly noted by his believed deity, and as such their transition to the afterlife will be joyous. We often fail to recognise this form of happiness as it repulses most of the human race, but it is certainly something that happens, even if the thought fills us with disgust. Like I have mentioned, the human body is a fragile structure. We aren't blessed with a strong defence against any sort of physical attack, because *"The human body lacks any particularly savage biological weapons, such as sharp claws or fangs, horns or spikes, poison glands or heavy jaws. Many other animals are well equipped, but the human species is a puny object by comparison, unable, in naked body-to-body combat, to inflict lethal injury without a great deal of effort"* (Morris, 2002: 232). Despite the fact that our bodies lack any of the aforementioned defence mechanisms, what we do have is the largest brain in the animal kingdom, and it's this 3lb of mass which has enabled us to shape society in a way that is alien in the rest of the animal kingdom.

As you have read, emotions play an integral role in everyday life due to their many variations, yet sometimes we forget that emotions affect everyone in different ways. Granted that the psychological effects of certain key emotions are almost the same for all humans (changes in heart rate when afraid, pupil dilation when attracted) but it is the trigger that isn't the same for everyone. What one person finds frightening, someone else might find humorous. I recall going to watch the film *'Paranormal Activity'* with a good friend many years back and being truly terrified, while he laughed and giggled his way through it. I thought that this was his way of dealing with fear, attempting to laugh it off as a precursor to avoid showing fear in front of others. Sadly, this wasn't the case, as he thought it was a comedy! I made no attempt to conceal my fear and he ridiculed me for months afterwards. However, put him in a room with 50 frogs and he would feel the same sensational terror I experienced during the movie, whereas I would be fine. We all experience emotions and some people are naturally more emotional than others, but it's how we manage those who experience emotions in front of us that is the challenge. Most displays of emotion are signals to other people that things are either great or not so great. These are polar opposite emotions that are instantly recognisable in the face and throughout a variety of body language channels.

However, I think the key emotion we often fail to show in this day and age is compassion. After chatting with many, many people I get the impression that compassion is becoming lost as many people in society have busier and busier lives. As mentioned, the current economic climate is making it increasingly more difficult for people to simply support their families so this has to be their focus and therefore, the needs of others outside of their immediate family become secondary. Having described watching so many people walk past a homeless man on a cold day reminded me that at times, we're so caught up in our own lives that we often forget about the wellbeing of others. Don't get me wrong, this isn't a witch hunt, but just think about

how you could perform just one simple act every once in a while that brings no benefit to yourself but momentarily brightens up the life of another person. One of my favourite quotes is by famous English writer Samuel Johnson, and it is *"the true measure of a man is how he treats someone who can do him absolutely no good"*.

Incidentally, in October 2013, UK Health Secretary Jeremy Hunt stated in a speech that it is a national shame that as many as 800,000 people are chronically lonely, which again harks back to my point about compassion being somewhat lacking in our busy society. He continued to say that *"each and every lonely person has someone who could visit them and offer companionship….(and there is) a forgotten million who live amongst us, ignored to our national shame"* (Daily Mail article, 2013).

One way to improve your ability to read the emotions of others is to look around you at a shopping centre. Some people might not be expressing any emotions at all, some might be full of emotion. Granted you might not be able to establish why they are experiencing an emotion, but at least you noticed it. This is how you'll become more adept at reading emotions, as by recognising them in other people, you become practised in reading the correct signals each emotion sends. We are going to be living on this planet for many more years to come, and granted we are a very peaceful race (the vast majority of us) but showing compassion to those less fortunate and reaching out to them is the best way to keep the peace for future generations.

The next chapter will look at how various emotions are tied in with the area of superstitions.

Chapter 2: Superstitions

The Fear of the unknown

A survey undertaken last year (2012) reported that 5.8 million people admit to being superstitious and 4.3 million claim to have a lucky number (see bibliography for full Daily Mail article).

During my research about what to include in this book, superstitions were the #1 choice of those questioned. I asked people (in person and also via my Facebook body language page, YouTube and email) whether they genuinely believe that superstitious beliefs play a significant role in human behaviour in today's modern society. The answer – to my surprise - was a resounding 'yes'. One area that has always fascinated me is the rise and popularity of superstitions, but more importantly, their noticeable effect on human behaviour and more specifically, on people's emotions. Much like the cultural body language differences that exist between cultures and places (as seen in my previous book), superstitions vary in both form and belief from place to place. After heeding undisputed public opinion, I first conducted research in my home town of Preston (England) about people's beliefs on superstitions and whether or not they believed in them, and if so, why they perform certain rituals. My findings categorically revealed that there are fascinating varieties of popular superstitions that feature in daily life, from eating out to travelling by air, and that even the world of sport has been infiltrated by superstitious beliefs and rituals. The results of my investigation now follow.

Research into superstitions

The very idea that an emotion can be triggered by a superstitious

Human Behaviour

belief is, in my opinion, very real, and has close links with the previous chapter. After chatting with a shop owner friend of mine, he informed me that once a year he is visited by a local gypsy traveller lady. The reason for this is that the gypsy wants him to buy a 'good luck' trinket from her which she believes has the power to last for one year. The shop owner told me that he doesn't believe in superstitions in general, however in this case, he has to buy one of her items because this tradition runs in his family. He told me that his family have always been quite fortunate with regards to luck, and he doesn't wish to 'jinx' himself or his family by breaking such a long-standing tradition. He also told me that he doesn't wish to find out if indeed the reason why his family have been fortunate is because of these trinkets – rather, he doesn't want to risk hampering that good fortune by not buying her items. Naturally this got me thinking about the very nature of superstitions, namely that if someone believes in one, or indeed a select few, then why doesn't that person believe in them all? Why do people pick and choose their superstitious beliefs? The vast majority of people I questioned could reel off a list of 5 or 6 superstitions that they believe ward off bad luck (popular ones included 'touching wood', avoiding walking under a ladder, not opening a umbrella inside and avoiding walking on 3 grids) and they could also give me a list of the superstitions that they didn't perform for whatever reason. On the flip side, they struggled to list many superstitions that they perform to bring themselves good luck (which I will discuss later on). Incidentally, as I moved from location to location and asked people for their thoughts about superstitions, they gave me a list of what they believed in; however this time, the ones that others had listed as not being credible were now being listed as popular beliefs.

I think one of the most important aspects I found during my research was that people who believe in superstitions often don't

Chapter 2: Superstitions

believe in a deity. This confused me, as those people who act out a superstition are in their own minds essentially eradicating themselves from bad luck or misfortune, which to me implies that they must believe in the presence of something 'unseen' which could cause the misfortune. They are purposely reducing the likelihood of whatever the consequence is for non-compliance. However, what about the flip side of this? If someone believes in bad luck, surely they must believe in the opposing good luck? However, nearly everyone I questioned found it difficult to think of more than 3 superstitions that bring good luck (finding 4 leafed clovers & touching wood being the most popular). Many people did also mention having a black cat cross your path, but most couldn't decide if that was good or bad luck. As an aside, black cats were traditionally thought to be witches' familiars, so if one crossed your path, it was believed that a witch had her eye on you, which was obviously seen as a bad luck omen.

What interests me is that if people believe in the power of bad luck, why don't people pray to a deity for good fortune? Surely you can't have one without the other? My research suggested that to believe in a deity is more far-fetched than believing that breaking a mirror will bring 7 years' bad luck. Think about how many times you've touched wood after saying something, crossed your fingers for someone, said 'white rabbits' first thing on the 1st day of the month or avoided walking on three grids or on cracks in the pavement. Some people perform these actions to avoid bad luck, and some are just forces of habit that serve no purpose, but are performed 'just in case'. Superstitions are a truly fascinating area of human behaviour and often form part of daily life without people being consciously aware of them.

Some of the more idiosyncratic superstitions I found during my research are as follows:

- I have an incredible fear of flying, so I believe if I touch the outside of the plane as I am boarding, then we won't crash. I make everyone I'm travelling with do this too.

- If you step on a crack (i.e. in the pavement) you'll break your mum's back.

- Drinking the water you use to boil an egg will bring you out in warts.

- All elephant figurines must face a window or a door or you will not reach your true destiny.

- It is bad luck to pass the salt.

Another aspect that was mentioned by those I questioned was the ancient art of Feng Shui, which is a system of organising your home or workspace to promote the flow of positive energy and to bring about good fortune, health and happiness. Advocates of Feng Shui believe that if positive energy flows smoothly in and out of all living and non-living things in a household, then the occupants will experience positive results in their personal and work lives. Interestingly, those who I talked to who believed in Feng Shui told me that superstitions in general are just pure nonsense, however they firmly believed that by practising Feng Shui they would gain good fortune. This goes to show that there is no agreement as to what actions can bring about good fortune, and it is down to the individual to decide what they believe in.

Emotional responses like fear and elation can in my opinion by triggered by a superstition. To believe in a superstition means you either a) fear the possibility of a punishment for non-compliance or b) you hope that by complying with it, you will bring success upon yourself. Yet interestingly, people who believe in certain superstitions often don't carry out other superstitions that they don't believe in, but they don't feel that this will in any way bring them bad luck. An example could be that one person may feel compelled to salute a magpie for fear of the consequences, yet this same person may have no problem in putting new shoes on the table. What I found during my research is that many people used certain superstitions during their daily life without being consciously aware of their words or actions. My hairdresser 'touched wood' (mentioned shortly) when she told me that she hoped next week would be busier than this week, and the till operator in my local Tesco told me that he'll 'keep his fingers crossed' for me that the lottery ticket I had just bought will be a winner. I remember my old personal trainer telling me to 'break a leg' when I was about to run a long road race, even though I thought that this was a good luck phrase only said to those about to perform on the stage. These examples have become figures of speech and have no real bearing on events, but are still performed without conscious thought with the hope of attracting good luck.

Superstitious rhymes, sayings and beliefs and their origins

During the course of your life, you will no doubt have heard many superstitious rhymes and sayings, and in this chapter I intend to shed some light on some of their often surprising origins. One superstitious rhyme that I found to have great prominence is the one related to the amount of magpies a person sees at any one time. A variation of this superstition is to salute every magpie you see using a hand gesture to the forehead and repeating the following words or a variation of them: "Good Morning Mr. Magpie, how is your lady wife today?" The rhyme reads as follows:

Human Behaviour

One for sorrow,

Two for joy,

Three for a girl,

Four for a boy,

Five for silver,

Six for gold,

Seven for a secret never to be told.

There is also a regional variation that exists and it continues the rhyme as follows:

Eight for a wish

Nine for a kiss

Ten for a surprise you should be careful not to miss

Eleven for health

Twelve for wealth

Thirteen beware it's the devil himself (I will cover superstitions linked to the number 13 later on)

I also found the rhyme itself does have many regional variations. When I asked people about the punishment they feared for failing to salute a magpie, the answers varied from person to person. Some believe that the magpie is the carrier of bad luck whereas others believe that magpies mate for life, so seeing one on its own is considered a sign of sorrow because it has lost its companion and therefore its misfortune will be passed on to you. Interestingly, if you delve further into this superstition, you will find that the urban legend behind the magpie is that they carry a drop of the Devil's blood under their tongue (seen as a harbinger of impending death) or that the reason the magpie is cursed is because it was alleged to be the only bird that didn't sing and comfort Jesus when he was crucified on the cross. Another belief is that the magpie can fly

Chapter 2: Superstitions

very high (i.e. in and out of heaven) and some believe that a magpie is The Devil in disguise, so if you acknowledge one by saying the greeting listed above, you are letting The Devil know that you have seen him sneaking around and he will leave you alone. As is the case with other common superstitions, this one has a variety of possibilities as to why it exists. It also plays strongly on people's emotion of fear – the fear of bringing bad luck upon themselves if they do not acknowledge the magpie each and every time they see one or more.

Interestingly, out of all the people I asked about the magpie superstition, not one person could tell me why the superstition exists and nor could they list the rest of the verse after the seventh line. I was astonished to hear that for something that has such a bearing on everyday life (the possibility of receiving bad luck) those who believe in this superstition do not wish to research why they religiously perform the act. Perhaps once they researched it, they might find greater reason to believe in the superstition, or maybe they will decide to let go of their belief in saluting magpies. That is the beauty of human behaviour - we often perform actions (much like the vast majority of the body language we display during daily life) without much thought as to why we do so. It is noteworthy that one of the most common reasons given as to why people perform superstitions was down to their upbringing. Childhood influences could play a huge role in the belief of some superstitious, as the majority of people I interviewed told me that it was their family's belief (often grandparents) which dictated whether they perform a particular superstition. What is very significant is that many people do not rid themselves of certain superstitious beliefs even when they reach their adult years. Children are taught from a very early age to believe in a variety of magical beings (Father Christmas, the Easter bunny, The Sandman and the Tooth Fairy), however by the time we reach adulthood, it is expected that we will all have outgrown our belief in these make-believe characters. This in some respects makes it quite curious that some fully-grown adults still believe in saluting a magpie yet would never still retain the belief that Santa Claus really exists. Despite the fact that the person may have matured both physically and mentally, there is still a fear within them that if they do not perform a certain ritual, bad luck will befall them. The superstition almost becomes a ritual, because people are unable to rid themselves of an act that 'could' bring about a spell of bad fortune.

"Something old, something new, something borrowed, something blue" is a rhyme that is commonly adhered to by brides on their wedding day, and the belief is that she must have something that corresponds to all of the categories otherwise she may have bad luck on her wedding day or in her future marriage. Interestingly, there is an extra line in this rhyme which reads "and a silver sixpence in her shoe" – the addition of the money is believed to bring the bride good financial fortune in the future.

Common superstitious beliefs linked to bad luck

> **It is bad luck to give someone a purse or wallet as a present without putting some money inside.** The superstition states that it is bad luck to do so because it will mean the receiver will be without money for the duration of time that they use the wallet or purse. Another superstition linked to purses and wallets is that it is bad luck to buy one for yourself. My sister was once in a shop and a lady came up to her with a £5 note and a purse in her hand, and asked my sister if she would be so kind as to go to the till and purchase the item on her behalf, as she explained that she felt it would be unlucky for her to do so herself.

Chapter 2: Superstitions

Additionally, once my sister had done as the lady had asked, she then passed my sister a pound coin to place in the purse so that she would not be receiving an empty purse. This example illustrates how seriously some people adhere to this superstition.

➢ **Never give anyone a pair of shoes as a Christmas gift.** This is a lesser-known superstition and I was actually unaware of it until I started doing my research for this book. It is thought that the shoes would make the receiver want to walk away from you, but I was unable to find the origin of this superstition.

➢ **Don't put new shoes on the table** is another fascinating superstition with a variety of possible origins, one of which goes back to the 18th century when men carried out particularly dangerous work (builders/miners etc). If a man died at work, his shoes were returned to his family and placed on the table as a symbol to show that the person had died. The reason his shoes were brought to his family was because shoes in those days were the one thing a man wore that could identify him clearly to his family without them having to see his body. Shoes were very unique (unlike they are today) and many people, especially those who were working class, only had a single pair which lasted a very long time through regular repairs. This act died out in the early 20th century and soon after became a superstition. Putting shoes on the table was (and may always will be) associated with the death of a loved one, so by doing so, it may be seen as tempting fate.

➢ **Never cross on the stairs.** This is said to originate from the time when people regularly had servants and they were not permitted to pass their masters on the stairs as this was considered rude and may result in the servant being dismissed. Another reason is that during the olden days, swords were carried on the belt, so a person crossing another on the stairs could have been impaled by their blade.

- **Don't open up an umbrella inside.** This superstition again has a variety of origins. The ancient Egyptians used umbrellas to keep dignitaries safe from the sun's burning rays, so opening an umbrella inside would offend the God of the Sun and bring bad luck to the person who did so. Another origin dates back to the 18th century, where Londoners used to have very large umbrellas which were spring-loaded. These were so large that if they were to be opened in the house, they might cause some serious damage or injure someone in the vicinity. This action was considered to be very disrespectful to the etiquette of that time and was regarded as very rude and certainly something to be avoided. The bad luck element was added to make people believe that such an action is superstitious.

1. **Never walk under a ladder** – In the Daily Mail article mentioned at the start of this chapter, this superstition came out as Britain's most popular. Apart from the obvious risk of something like a tin of paint falling on your head, there are 3 other believed origins of this superstition:

2. The way the ladder leans against the wall was supposed to resemble the gallows, so if you walked under the ladder, you could be almost guaranteeing that you'd end your days this way.

Chapter 2: Superstitions

3. The ancient Egyptians believed that a special power was held by the triangle shape that the ladder makes when leant against a wall, so if a person was to walk under it, they would be seen as breaking its power.

4. Finally, a ladder used to be leant up against the gallows in order to cut down the dead body after hanging, so if you walk under a ladder, you are risking being hit by the body.

➢ **Smashing a mirror brings seven years' bad luck** – The Daily Mail article again states that around 9 million people believe this long-standing superstition. This belief can be traced back to the Romans who were the first to create glass mirrors. They (along with Greek, Chinese, African and certain Indian cultures) believed that the mirror had the power to confiscate part of the user's soul, so therefore if the reflected image became distorted in any way (e.g. through breakage) then this would result in the soul becoming corrupted. Furthermore, the Romans believed that a person's physical body renewed itself every seven years, so the unlucky person would have to wait for this set period of time before their soul could be fully restored. The belief was that the unfortunate person who had broken the mirror would have an incomplete soul which would be incapable of warding off evil spirits, hence why they would suffer one incident of misfortune after another. Interestingly, it is said that if you are unfortunate enough to break a mirror, you can counteract the bad luck by burying the pieces in your garden by moonlight.

➢ **Friday the 13th** – This date has been seen as unlucky for many years and there is even an official name for a specific phobia of this date – *paraskevidekatriaphobia*. It is interesting to note that in the Bible, many negative events happened on a Friday such as Eve tempting Adam with the forbidden fruit, the start of the Great Flood, the destruction of the Temple of Solomon and more significantly of course, the crucifixion of Christ himself. These events demonstrate that there may well have been a long standing association between Fridays and bad luck, and when you combine Friday with the number 13 – which has its own set of bad luck associations covered later – the effect is magnified.

Common superstitious beliefs linked to good luck

- ➤ ***Horseshoe*** – When facing upwards, this is believed to bring good luck because it is supposed to capture and hold onto any good luck which happens to be floating by. People who subscribe to this belief will place an upturned horseshoe on the outside of their house or stable to ensure good luck for the occupants within. The opposite is said to be true of a horseshoe with the ends pointing downwards – the good luck is said to literally fall out. An alternative view is that when upturned, the horseshoe resembles the devil's horns, so it should be inverted to allow the devil to run out of it. Morris (1999) offers a further variation of this superstition, namely that when the horseshoe is on its side, it resembles the letter C for Christ and therefore offers Christian protection. Finally, in ancient times, iron was far more rare and precious than it is today, so much so that people believed it was endowed with supernatural powers, so that may account for why people believed the iron horseshoe could bring good luck.

- ➤ **Saying "white rabbits" on the first day of the month.**

This is believed to bring good luck for all of the coming month, but it must be said first thing in the morning before any other words are spoken to have its full effect. Some people take this superstition a step further and have to say the word 'rabbits' three times first thing in the morning, with others also saying 'black rabbits' last thing at night on the last day of the month. But if they then got muddled and said 'black rabbits' in the morning instead of 'white', then a month of bad luck would follow. The origin of this superstition is vague but it has been mentioned in literature as far back as 1909, so it is at least 100 years old. One possible reason for saying this particular word is that rabbits have a history of being regarded as lucky animals (hence why some people carry a rabbit's foot to bring good luck, which, as an aside, is because many years ago, witches were said to take the form of a rabbit, so by carrying around the paw of one, it was a sign that you'd slain a witch). Also, white rabbits in the wild are rarer than grey or brown ones, so you would have to be especially lucky to see one. Another aspect worth mentioning is that some people believe that rabbits can literally jump into the future and bring happiness and good luck.

➢ ***Finding a four leaf clover*** – This is one of the most popular good luck charms, and indeed, in the United States, around four million four-leaf clovers are encased in glass or plastic and sold as lucky charms every year (Morris, 1999). Some Christians believe this item can bring good luck because the sacred cross also has four parts, but others believe each of the four leaves is supposed to stand for hope, faith, love and luck. The luck part is only connected to the fourth leaf, hence why no good luck is obtained after

Human Behaviour

finding a three leaf clover. The exception to this would be the three-leaf clover or Shamrock, which is a very common protective symbol in Ireland. The Irish believe that this symbol brings them good luck and protection from ills as St. Patrick himself is supposed to have demonstrated that the three leaves represent the Holy Trinity. According to legend, if you find a four leaf clover you should place it in your shoe or in a Bible for safekeeping. Finally, as Morris also describes, there is a rhyme linked to finding a four-leaf clover that reads as follows " *'one leaf for fame, one leaf for wealth, one leaf for a faithful lover and one leaf to bring you glorious health are all in the four leaf clover'. In this way, this sums up all the greatest fears of the vulnerable human being… and if a humble little plant can help to avoid such major disasters then it is not surprising that enterprising salesmen can dispense with four million of them a year"* (1999: 113)

➢ **Touch wood** – this is done when a person wants to a) prevent something negative from happening to them again, as seen in the example "I've had three colds already this month – touch wood I won't get a fourth" or b) because they hope that something good happens to them shortly, as seen in the example "I've had lots of wins on the scratchcards lately – touch wood it continues". The origin of why we actually touch wood could be linked to the Pagan belief that good spirits like fairies live in trees and therefore by knocking on wood, you are summoning them to come out of the tree and grant your wish. Others believe that by knocking on wood, you are making it difficult for the bad tree-dwelling spirits to hear what you are saying, so as such, they won't be able to interfere and bring you bad luck. Alternatively, some Christians believe that by touching

Chapter 2: Superstitions

wood, you are touching a representation of the cross of Christ and so as such, you are seeking his protection. What is most interesting about this saying is that there are variations of it found all over the world, and both the Arabs and the Brazilians have a saying which translates as 'knock on wood'. Similar variations occur in Sweden, Finland, Trinidad and Tobago and the USA, which just demonstrates the close association that wood has with the bringing of luck or the avoidance of misfortune.

➢ **"See a penny, pick it up, and all that day you'll have good luck".** There is a tradition of pennies bringing good luck, possibly going back to the time when metals were precious (and some even believed them to be a gift from the Gods), so picking one up was seen to bring good luck. In some areas, there is an extension to the rhyme which is as follows "find a penny upside down, all day long you'll wear a frown". By upside down, this means that the penny would be heads-down i.e. tails up, and the belief that finding a coin like this (and picking it up) could lead to bad luck is all linked to a long-standing belief in the battle between good (heads) and evil (tails). Tradition has it that if you should find such a coin, you should turn it over (so it's heads up) to let someone else find it and have good luck.

Charms and Amulets

In the summer of 2013 I took a research trip to the historic locations of Whitby and York to investigate first-hand the power of superstitious beliefs. Both places are steeped in history and I wanted to learn more about some of the protective amulets and charms which are prevalent in these places. Upon my arrival to Whitby, I was amazed by how many shops sell necklaces adorned with so-called 'healing crystals'. I entered one busy marketplace and was inundated with a variety of good luck charms, amulets and other trinkets which are designed to ward off bad luck. I got chatting with one such stall owner who informed me that people from all over the world come to her shop and buy certain amulets which have a greater significance in their home country than they do here in the UK, such as the Acorn. The Acorn is believed to be a bringer of luck and prosperity, to offer protection from lightning and to increase sexual potency, and is attributed to the Norse God, Thor. In some parts of ancient Germany, Scandinavia and England, the oak was believed to be favoured by Thor. Yet not all protective amulets are universal and some have a variety of meanings. Incredibly, the stall owner told me that some of her customers are unable to start their day without holding, touching or attaching their good luck amulet to their person.

The popular amulet that originates from Whitby is the Adder Stone, which is sometimes also known as the snake stone or St. Hilda's stone. Legend has it that St. Hilda (a seventh century abbess) tried to build her abbey on the clifftops of Whitby but was prevented by the venomous snakes that inundated the grasslands around the top. As such, St. Hilda used special prayers and magic spells which made the snakes curl up into spirals and roll off the cliff face onto the beach below, therefore allowing her to successfully build her abbey. From then on, representations of their fossilized remains have been used as protective amulets to ward off various illnesses such as whooping cough, fever and eye diseases (Morris, 1999).

Interestingly, superstitions do vary from place to place, and also in their intensity. For instance, a deep-rooted superstition from the Mediterranean is called the 'evil eye' and this is the belief that some people have this negative affliction, and whoever they make eye contact with will suffer from bad luck. Such is the power of this belief, people will go to great lengths to eradicate themselves from the possibility of attracting the attention of the evil eye by wearing brightly coloured amulets around their neck or wrist (especially eye amulets). This is because it is proposed that the bright colours will distract the gaze of those who have the evil eye and prevent them from making eye contact with the recipient and therefore, this will block the bad luck from being passed onto them. This tradition is also commonly seen in fishermen who adorn their boats with symbolic 'eye' adornments to fend off bad luck whilst at sea and also, some people place trinkets in their houses to avoid any bad luck being passed on should they be visited by an unwelcome stranger who may have the evil eye.

In addition, the Turkish Blue Eye bead is believed by natives of Turkey to also offer protection from the evil eye (and general bad fortune) and it is often worn as an item of jewellery, hung in a car or carried round as a key chain. Linked to this is The Hand of Fatima which is a protective charm popular in the Middle East. In the Arabic world it is known as the Hamsa Hand because 'Hamsa' means 'five' in a reference to the number of digits on the hand. These amulets feature a flat downward facing hand and are believed to bring good luck to the wearer and bestow upon them the virtues of patience and faithfulness. Some also have an eye symbol somewhere on the hand (usually on the palm) which offers additional protection from the evil eye.

St. Christopher

The icon of St. Christopher is used on many items of jewellery even today and sometimes, the wearer may be unaware of its significance. He is the Patron Saint of travellers and so, by wearing an item of jewellery containing his image, it is supposed to offer to the wearer safety when travelling. In 1969 however, church authorities removed him from the official list of Saints due to some speculation regarding the fact that he could have been entirely fictitious, and his Saint's day (25th July) vanished from the calendar (Morris, 1999)

You may also be interested to learn that *"in 1968, contractors working on the Vanguard rocket project for the United States Navy blamed a series of failures on the absence of St. Christopher medals on the rockets. A medal was attached to the next rocket and it worked perfectly"* (Webster, 2008: 54). You must decide if this was just pure coincidence or not.

Peacock feathers

Many people believe that peacock feathers bring bad luck, as the eye on the feather is supposed to be the evil eye. What is noteworthy however is that a superstition can differ across cultures as for instance in India, people make fans out of peacock feathers – not to keep themselves cool, but rather because they believe the eyes on the feathers actually look out for evil and ward it off. They have a similar meaning in China and Japan but certainly not in the West, where they are considered by many to be most unlucky and some people would refuse to have them in their house. Whilst on my research trip to Whitby I found many shops selling peacock feather charms, so this goes to show that some people in the UK must also believe in their power to ward off bad luck otherwise the shop would not stock them if nobody bought them.

Full moon

A full moon is also linked to a whole range of superstitions, and not just the ones depicted on the silver screen such as werewolves and zombies. Indeed, the term 'lunatic' derives from the Latin word 'luna' meaning 'moon', and the term was often used to describe the way that the behaviour of inmates in a lunatic asylum became worse during a full moon. Some believe this change in behaviour is because the body is made up of approximately 50-65% water and the moon has a gravitational pull on water i.e. via the tides, so by default we are likely to be affected by the full moon.

A nurse friend of mine refuses to work a shift on a full moon because of the increase in difficult behaviour from the patients, and a study conducted by the Sussex police force showed an increase in violent crime during a full moon. A police officer responsible for the research stated that *'from my 19 years experience of being a police officer, undoubtedly on full moons we do tend to get people with sort of strange behaviour: more fractious & argumentative'* (Daily Mail article, 5th June 2007). Brighton Police force also announced in 2007 that they were going to deploy more officers during a full moon, and a study published by German scientists in 2000 claimed the full moon also sparked a rise in binge drinking (see article in bibliography). They checked the police arrest reports and blood-alcohol tests of 16,495 offenders, and most of those with an excess of 2ml of alcohol per 100ml of blood - drunk, under German law - had been caught during the five-day full moon cycle.

Another study published in 1998 discovered a rise in violent incidents among the 1,200 inmates at Armley Jail in Leeds during the days either side of a full moon. Furthermore, it has been proven by a leading insurer in the UK that there is a 14% rise in car accidents during a full moon compared to a new moon, and this study was based on the analysis of 3 million car policies (Bloomberg article, 2003). This could suggest that people's behaviour becomes more erratic and that they take more risks when the moon is full for reasons not yet fully understood.

Human Behaviour

To me, the effect of the moon on the human body is more than just a superstition, because people have studied this area and have found more than just tenuous links. Very recently, a study showed a link between sleep and a full moon, namely that in a study of 33 volunteers, many took 5 minutes longer to fall asleep and experienced reduced sleep quality (20 minutes' fewer sleep) during a full moon and furthermore, participants received 30% less deep sleep which is the most important type as the body needs this time to repair itself. Some believe that lighter sleep during a full moon would have helped to protect our cave-dwelling ancestors. Granted this study was quite small (33 participants) but the results were quite conclusive.

Another recent study quoted in an online article on the Daily Mail's website analysed the behaviour of 771 people admitted to a psychiatric unit in Canada and found that admissions were no more likely during a full moon. Yet conversely, this finding was in sharp contrast to the views of 63% of doctors and 80% of nurses in the same study who stated that they saw more patients with mental health problems during a full moon than at any other time. This example just goes to show that the effect of the full moon on humans is by no means conclusive and is open to much speculation.

The Ouija Board

Interestingly, during my research into superstitions, those linked to the Ouija Board quickly gained my attention. Some people told me that they don't believe in superstitions or in the bad luck they claim to bring for non-compliance. However, as soon as I asked if they believed in the superstition of the Ouija board, their responses were totally different and almost unanimously negative. I am acutely aware of the difference between the paranormal and a superstition,

Chapter 2: Superstitions

however I wanted to learn more about people's beliefs about the unknown. Some of those I questioned about this topic shared their experiences with me via my Facebook page and gave me their permission to share these in this book.

"My friend's mum and dad did it.. Her dad was sceptical, until that is they contacted a relative on her side who didn't like him and a glass flew across the room and smashed in front of his face - one said a spirit never left the house afterwards .. The other said two days afterwards, "someone" pushed them down the stairs. I wouldn't risk it! (i.e. using a Ouija board) "

"A work colleague told me that before she moved house, she and her friends messed about with the Ouija board. She felt as if there was an evil presence there and it even followed her to her new house because it became very heavy and depressing. Another story mum told me was when she was a kid, her friends had the board and were trying to make contact and the thing kept moving to the alphabet like crazy and whatever it was hit the mirror and went straight out of window, breaking it. They were terrified and never spoke of it for years"

"I have used one myself but it was done properly through a medium when myself and my friends went to a York museum haunted night group experience. I was wary about it but the medium assured me it's safe with her being there, and having a gold ring inside the glass stops evil spirits breaking free. It was about a young girl who had been murdered back in the 1800's, it was a weird sensation because I was sceptical of this at first.... it's like a buzzing feeling in your fingertip. There were about 5 of us - we all put our fingers lightly on the glass and it moved not long after we asked "anyone here?" It was a young girl that had been murdered by this guy she befriended, think she was only about 17, lost and sad. When others took their fingers off the glass, I was just about to take mine off but mine and Rachel's fingers wouldn't move off the glass – it was as if they were stuck like glue. This freaked me out a bit and Rachel said the same and the glass moved again as if she wanted to carry on talking and said Goodbye. It was weird and it scared me cos my finger was stuck"

The limited research I conducted into Ouija boards was however quite conclusive, and I'm sure if you were to question people you know about the board, you would find that opinion about them is overwhelmingly negative. Most people I discussed this subject with told me they would never play on a Ouija board and no amount of money would make them change their mind. It's interesting that some people who don't believe in superstitions (often used to fend off evil spirits/paranormal) still would never use the board. They are accepting that there is something paranormal with the Ouija board which should not be messed with, yet they believe a superstition in general is purely psychological nonsense.

Modern internet-based superstitions Superstitions research

The beauty about human behaviour is that we're always learning. I had almost concluded this chapter on superstitions when I received a forwarded email from an old friend. It contained strict instructions that I had to forward it on to 13 other friends by midnight or the punishment would be bad luck for 1 year. In my eagerness to learn more about some traditional superstitions, I had been oblivious to the new modern 'chain letter' style emails/forwarded messages that exploit people's fear of superstitions. As my Facebook page (*Understanding Body Language: Liars, Cheats and Happy feet*) has many thousands of followers from a variety of different cultures and backgrounds, I felt that this would be a good starting place to conduct some research about superstitions that are linked to chain-letter style email/Facebook posts. I had a good response, as many people reported receiving or viewing such posts and I will now analyse some of the more interesting responses, starting with the following.

"I ignore these but they do play with my emotions and leave

me thinking – What if I don't forward this message on - will I not have good luck? Even though I know this is exactly the desired effect and my luck, fortune etc won't change if I don't forward a message or re-post, for a split second the emotion of fear in some form does surface before the logical thinking process"

I think this lady has managed to encapsulate the feelings of many when they receive or view such messages, and indeed, the overwhelming majority of the respondents did not follow the orders contained within the messages to forward/share them, and indeed likened them to emotional blackmail.

"I see a lot of these posts from the same two or three people. I actually un-friended a few in the past because its spam to me – I feel disappointed in people who send them and would never forward. It's junk cluttering my timeline coupled with an attempt to manipulate through emotional blackmail."

This lady makes a valid point – that in fact, you may very well feel disappointed that a) a certain friend of yours has sent you this message in the 1st place, therefore showing that they have fallen for the blackmail contained within e.g. forward to 10 friends today or else xyz will happen to you and b) that this particular friend is now putting pressure on you to not only send the message back to then, but also for you to send it to 10 more friends. After interviewing many people here in Lancashire, I was truly astonished when some people reported that if a friend sent them either a text or an email telling them they had to forward the message onto their friends (to create a chain) then they would agree to do it. Again, as technology has advanced, so have superstitions – they have become portable and can be accessed from anywhere in the world. For instance, now you can be sat in the comfort of your own home mindlessly

Human Behaviour

watching television and you could be pestered via email to forward a certain message on to as many people as possible or risk bringing a number of years' worth of bad luck upon yourself. Granted that these messages aren't an actual superstition in their own right, yet they do provide the receiver with a psychological conundrum. Do they ignore the enclosed message and run the risk of non-compliance, or agree and send the message on so as to avoid the punishment that they fear their non-compliance may bring?

Superstitions have even infiltrated the social media world of Facebook. Only this morning, whilst checking my newsfeed, one of my friends shared a postcard with a picture of a $50 bill on it with text that read: **"In October there are 5 Mondays, 5 Tuesdays and 5 Wednesdays. This happens once every 823 years. This is called money bags. So share this as your status and money will arrive within 4 days. Based on Chinese Feng Shui. The one who does not share, will be without money. Copy within 11 mins of reading."**

You may be surprised to learn that this post (as of Nov '13) has had 494,019 shares and 68,626 likes! What is even more unbelievable is that the post is factually incorrect, because the 1st Oct 2013 fell on a Tuesday, meaning there are only 4 Mondays in the month. Also, there is another misleading error in the text – this occurrence of 5 Mondays, Tuesdays and Wednesdays in one month does not happen as infrequently as once every 823 years – this was just added in by the author to panic people into thinking it is such a rare event that they wouldn't want to risk missing it. Most people who see this post will just take it as read that the information it contains is correct and if they believe it, they will share it to avoid being without money (and I think that the author of this post has added in a mention of Feng Shui in order to give more credibility to the concept). In these austere times where money is in short supply,

Chapter 2: Superstitions

people's lives are difficult enough ordinarily, so they are less likely to risk bringing bad luck upon themselves and more likely just to share the post and not take the risk. You would think that only certain people would believe in such threats which exploit their insecurities and fears, however the number of shares/likes shows that the fear of financial difficulties is widespread and common. It is an issue that concerns people the world over because those who had commented on the post were spread all over the globe, and the author of the post would have known that choosing this subject would ensure maximum publicity. One possible reason as to why people create posts such as the one above is that they could encourage people to add the creator as a Facebook friend or to follow them, and for some people, the more Facebook friends they have, the more their ego is boosted and the more popular they feel. As Dale Carnegie states *"You want the approval of those with whom you come in contact…you want a feeling that you are important in your own little world"* (1981:97).

This showed me that even though we consider ourselves to be a fairly advanced nation in terms of our educational levels and access to new technology, examples such as this still appeal to people's deepest fears about inadvertently bringing bad luck upon themselves. Other examples I have seen on Facebook have included sharing pictures of lucky Buddhas, four leaf clovers and angels in order to bring good luck upon yourself and your family. Unfortunately, some of these posts take things a step further by using a more blatant example of blackmail. For instance, on a friend's wall, I read a list of horoscope personality descriptions billed as 'the most accurate you will ever read', but what was more questionable were the sentences above the horoscope which read:

'This is the real deal. Try ignoring it and the first thing you'll notice is that you'll have a horrible day starting tomorrow

morning, and it'll only get worse from there'.

This sentence was obviously slotted into this post by the creator in an attempt to gain lots of shares of their horoscopes, and also, underneath each star sign's description, it has sentences which read '12 years of bad luck if you do not share this post'. People who are prone to believing such threats will then share it with their friends in an attempt to avoid bringing any bad luck upon themselves and this in turn ensures wide coverage of the post for the author, giving them a desired and intentional boost to their popularity.

Text messages can also be used to prey on people's desire to always have good luck. My sister described to me a chain letter style text that she received last year, which read **"You are one of my special 10 friends. You are a special and unique friend. You are now on the clock – you have to forward this message to 10 other women you consider as a friend in the next ten minutes (and send it back to me if you consider me as a friend) or you will have a year of bad luck – GO!!"** My sister does not believe in chain letters but this made things a little awkward because if she had sent a copy of the message back to the original sender as requested by them, she would have been getting involved with the chain message which she did not agree with. This is the trouble with these modern superstitions – they end up being passed around from person to person in order to keep the peace, as one person, despite not believing in the content of the text/email, feels obliged to forward it on to avoid the sender thinking that the recipient has not complied with the terms of the message (and for instance, does not class them as a friend). The recipient fears that the sender will be waiting for them to forward a copy of the message back to them in order to re-affirm their friendship, and this plays on the receiver's emotions.

Chapter 2: Superstitions

Stones and superstitions

Many crystals or semi-precious stones are traditionally thought to help with a number of problems such as depression, insomnia, phobias and stress, and many books have been written on the subject. However, some are more closely associated with bad luck, and I'll cover some of the more common ones here:

Pearls

Some women believe that wearing pears is unlucky, which may be linked to the belief that the pearl represents the tear of the oyster who had to shed tears in order to make the pearl, as the pearl originated as a grain of sand that entered the oyster, irritated it and caused it to create a defensive secretion around the grain that then became the pearl. The superstition continues with the belief that women in love should particularly avoid wearing them so as not to bring bad luck (i.e. something that would cause the shedding of tears) upon their relationship. It is particularly unlucky for a bride to wear pearls on her wedding day for same reason.

Opals

The commonly-held belief is that if this is not your birthstone (i.e. if you were not born in October) then wearing opal jewellery will bring you bad luck. This superstition may have gained prominence because in a novel by Sir Walter Scott in 1829, the owner of an opal suffered nothing but bad luck. It is also known as the Rainbow stone due to the many colours that can be seen in it, but these colour variations may be why they are not popular to be given as a gift to one's partner (as they are not a symbol of constancy). The bad luck supposedly brought by the opal can be offset if the piece of jewellery also has diamonds in it, as they are supposed to overpower the opals. Some also believe that opals turn pale in the presence of a poison and lose their shine when their owners die.

Diamonds

Diamonds have long since been considered to bring about protection from many ills such as insanity, failure and weakness, and their powers are believed to be more potent if the diamond is given as a gift rather than being bought for oneself. They are also commonly used in engagement rings as they are supposed to have the power to increase the love felt between a man and a woman.

Traditionally revered by women as a 'girl's best friend', the diamond also has a darker side. A certain famous example of this stone named the 'Hope diamond' was said to bring exceptional bad fortune upon all those who had it in their possession —misfortunes such as financial ruin, suicide, death by drowning and marriage collapse have all befallen various people who have had this diamond in their possession (Morris, 1999).

Sports stars and superstitions

It is quite remarkable to think that the high level of intensity to which most modern athletes condition themselves to can be totally undone by the power of superstition. Most modern-day athletes have at their disposal state of the art training devices and software designed to aid performance, fitness and speed (and assist with recovery), yet incredibly, despite the body being a well-oiled machine, the mind can still believe that certain actions and beliefs can influence play either positively or negatively.

I have undertaken research and found a surprising number of popular sports stars who have a variety of rituals that they must perform either before, during or after their games. These beliefs play on their emotions, because they believe that if they do not perform them, they will not win. It is important to make the distinction between a common superstition performed to bring good luck (e.g. touching wood or saying 'white rabbits' on the 1st of the month) and the almost ritualistic routines performed by certain sports stars in order to improve performance. I will cover some very well-known sports stars and their own unique superstitions below:

Tennis

An award-winning Australian sports writer by the name of Will Swanton (2013) followed Rafael Nadal and other tennis stars over the course of a year and wrote a book describing his findings. He found that this superstar and multi-title winning tennis player has to perform a wide variety of ritualistic actions before and during a match (described below):

> *He must have a cold shower 45 minutes before a match.*
>
> *He must carry one racquet on to the court.*
>
> *He must have five other racquets in his bag.*
>
> *He must have wrapped his own white grip on his racquets in the locker room.*
>
> *His bag must be placed next to his chair on a towel, never on the chair.*
>
> *He must sprint to the baseline after the spin of the coin, perform a split-step and then a jog around the back court.*
>
> *He must towel down between every point. It can be ace or double fault - he must towel down as if he is covered in sweat.*
>
> *He must run his hair behind both ears.*
>
> *He must touch his nose.*
>
> *He must pick at his underpants.*
>
> *He must drink from two water bottles at changeovers. One bottle has cold water, one is warm.*

He must face the labels of his drink bottles to the end he is about to play from.

He must never rise from his seat before his opponent.

He must wait at the net post so his opponent can reach his seat first.

He must never walk on the sidelines as if he is avoiding cracks in the pavement.

On clay, he must run his foot along the plastic baseline on the side of the court he is about to play from.

At the Australian Open, when going from one side of the court to the other, he must walk across the MELBOURNE sign.

He must have his socks at the exact same height.

He must fold his towels after every changeover.

He cannot step on any lines on the court.

After reading this list (which is exhausting to read, never mind to perform) it does beg the question as to where a superstition ends and an obsession begins. The performing of such a regimented and detailed set of rituals is bordering on an anxiety disorder known as Obsessive Compulsive Disorder, where the sufferer firmly believes that they have to perform a fixed set of actions otherwise there will be a negative outcome. One of my college friends had to put his bathroom light on and off 77 times each morning before leaving the house otherwise he felt that his house would burn down. Other rituals include washing the hands many times (sometimes making the hands red raw) after touching anything that the sufferer believes contains germs, or a person being compelled to count the number of panes of glass in every building they walk past on the street. Many people are compelled to check many times if their front door is locked, because as this is often such an automatic thing to do, it is sometimes easy to forget whether you've actually performed the action or if you just thought about doing it.

Chapter 2: Superstitions

Rafael Nadal's rituals are a long way from just simply touching wood to bring good luck, but to him, they are not optional – he is strongly compelled to do them otherwise he believes he would lose a match. One could argue that these rituals for Rafael have become part of a self-fulfilling prophecy, because if a match official banned him from performing any of them, he would most likely become very stressed which would then affect his focus and concentration and would probably result in him losing the match. Consequently, he would blame this loss on the fact that he didn't perform his routines, therefore adding weight to his already steadfast belief that they help him to win. The extraordinary list of actions Rafael must perform also affect his opponent and the timing of the match itself – the player is expected to start play within 25 seconds of the umpire announcing 'time', but due to the number of rituals he must perform, this is often not possible within the time limit.

Rafael's superstitious beliefs are at the extreme end of the spectrum, yet many other sports have examples of players who perform rituals which they believe bring them good luck and help them win. I will cover a few below:

Golf

The world-famous golfer Tiger Woods has a superstition whereby he always wears red when playing a tournament on a Sunday, which first started when he was at college and he always wore red on the final day of any events. It is also reported that his Thai mother once told him that this is his lucky colour. Whilst researching the superstitions of golfers, I realised that they are quite widespread, with some players quoted as saying that they won't play with a ball marked higher than a 4 (so much so that manufacturers have stopped making them) and another famous golfer Ernie Els is quoted as saying that every ball only has one birdie in it, so after he

Human Behaviour

has achieved this score with one ball, he discards it and gets a new one (Northern Californian Golf Association website).

Rugby

One would ordinarily think that Rugby players would be very unlikely to believe that performing certain superstitious rituals would enhance performance, because one thinks of them as big, strong, masculine individuals. However, this is not necessarily the case, because as you would expect, many players would refuse to wear the number 13 jersey (but, much like the peacock feather superstition mentioned, this has a dual meaning, because the French rugby players actually argue over who is going to wear this jersey as it is seen as lucky).

A more bizarre superstition is linked to French player Christian Califano who is alleged to put a banana in his boot the week before a big game, possibly to bring good luck in a match – but one can only speculate at the state of the banana come match day!

The traditional ancestral war dance called the Haka has been performed by the New Zealand national rugby team before every match for the past 100 years, and it has been called the greatest ritual in world sport. One would have to speculate that the players believe it will enhance their performance in the game, as the fighting moves contained within the dance would get the adrenaline flowing. It has been criticised however as being an attempt to intimidate the opposition though, who have sometimes been reported to ignore it. Granted, the Haka is not a superstition as such, but I'm sure that there would be uproar from the New Zealand team if it was suggested that they should scrap performing it at the start of a match, because again, if they were then to lose this match, it would be blamed upon the absence of the Haka.

Chapter 2: Superstitions

Cricket

South African cricketer Neil McKenzie is reported to have certain rituals that he has to perform before a match which are linked to his fear of germs – he has to tape down the toilet lids in the changing rooms so that germs don't 'fly' out and he often tapes his bat to the ceiling so that germs can't attach to it. This behaviour developed into OCD and he spent several years trying to overcome the disorder. This example also shows that some sports stars' rituals are not performed solely to bring good luck, as some may be compelled to carry out certain actions because they are in the grips of a compulsive disorder.

Former England wicket keeper Jack Russell was well known for his superstitious nature, so much so that he refused to replace his hat and wicket keeping pads throughout his career in the belief that they brought him good luck. Also, he would always have two Weetabix for his lunch during a match, and they had to be soaked in milk for precisely eight minutes.

Former cricket umpire David Shepherd was known for his habit of hopping around on one leg whenever the score reached 111, 222, 333, etc as these numbers are said to be a bad omen for cricketers because the figures "111" resemble a wicket without bails. The number 111 is therefore known as 'Nelson', after Lord Nelson, who allegedly only had one eye, one arm and one testicle.

Finally, ex-Australian cricket captain Steve Waugh always carried a lucky red rag in his hip pocket ever since a match in 1993 when he used it as a sweat gatherer and shortly afterwards, scored a century. He also has a tatty old green cap that he refuses to throw away as he believes it brings him good luck.

Football

Human Behaviour

The Ivorian footballer Kolo Toure has a superstition whereby he must be the last player from his team on the pitch. Quite amusingly, there was one match whereby one of his team mates was having medical treatment in the changing room, and because he was waiting for him, Toure ended up bounding onto the pitch after the match had started and was booked by the referee.

Footballer John Terry admitted to the newspaper *The Mirror* that he has around 50 superstitions that he has to perform before the start of every match, which vary from listening to the same CD in the car on the way to a match, parking his car in the same spot, sitting in the same seat on the team bus and tying the tapes around his socks three times. He even wore the same lucky shin pads for ten years before losing them at an away game in Barcelona.

Ice Hockey

A firm believer in the power of superstition was Patrick Roy, one of the greatest goaltenders in the history of the game. Before each game, he would skate backwards towards his own net before turning around at the last second, because by doing so, he believed this would make the goal shrink. Also, when a puck was deflected from his net, he would thank the posts.

NFL

An American survey of almost 10,000 adult NFL fans conducted in October 2013 by alcoholic beverage maker Bud Light found that one of the most superstitious groups of fans (out of 32 teams in total) are those supporting the Baltimore Ravens. Many fans always perform certain rituals before watching a game, such as washing their car or eating the same meal, and during the game, many of them wear the same set of clothes each time and all the members of their family have to sit in the same place for every match of the

Chapter 2: Superstitions

season. What is interesting about this is the fact that because they are a good team, they frequently win, so naturally the fans would say that the reason for this is down to the rituals that they often perform, so this is yet another example of a superstition becoming a self-fulfilling prophecy. 37% of Ravens' fans believe that their superstitious rituals will affect the outcome of a game and 25% believe that not completing their superstitions will make the team miss a winning field goal or touchdown (see the bibliography for the full article).

Restaurant superstitions

Superstitious beliefs have even made their mark on the restaurant industry, as I will now describe. Kat and I enjoyed a recent trip to the popular Mexican restaurant chain Chiquito, and upon entering the building, I was immediately asked by the waitress if I would like to rub the head of their gecko statue for good luck. Despite thinking that it more closely resembled a Komodo dragon, I proceeded to ask her why this was considered to be lucky, but she didn't know. After conducting some research, it does appear that the gecko is considered to bring good fortune in certain cultures (such as in Hawaii and some of the Pacific islands), however at this present time I am unable to find out why rubbing the head of a gecko is considered to bring good luck. Perhaps this superstitious ritual was created by Chiquito's founders as a marketing stunt, because if customers believed that this gecko was indeed blessed with good fortune, then it would make sense to keep on revisiting the restaurant to eat and to rub the lucky Gecko's head to ensure their continued good fortune.

After we enjoyed a lovely meal, I contacted Chiquitos directly to find out the origin of this superstitious belief, and the reply I was given was *"Nobody knows where the story came from, Craig, but it is part of the Chiquito legend and we always feel a bit of luck never does you any harm."* This notion of a superstition being invented which has no basis on any particular fact links in well with what Dr. Desmond Morris said about organised religion in an interview he gave for the Huffington Post in 2012. He is quoted as saying *"religion is institutionalised superstition. Science has demonstrated the folly of basing decisions on superstitious beliefs. We should have got past that phase by now".* It is of course up to you the reader to decide whether or not you agree with Dr. Morris' controversial viewpoint.

Interestingly, after conducting further research into this superstition and checking their Facebook page, Chiquitos had asked their Facebook followers on May 20th 2013 if anyone had rubbed their lucky gecko Diago's head, and if they did, did they receive any good luck. The first thing I noticed was that this post got significantly more likes (190 at the time of writing) than most of the other posts on their wall, which were generally getting below 20 likes. This shows that people are interested in the concept of the gecko bringing good luck, as it got almost ten times the normal amount of likes. Six people out of the twenty five that commented on the post reported that nothing good had happened to them after rubbing the statue, and six reported that something good had happened, which ranged from stating that they had won money on the lottery, had received a tax refund and that their boyfriend had proposed to them afterwards. The remaining 13 comments were not of much significance. Obviously it is by no means conclusive that this statue does bring good luck – maybe if fifty different people had reported good luck then the action of rubbing the gecko may have had more credibility. Indeed, the waitress who greeted us as we entered the restaurant asked if we would like to rub the gecko's head for good luck and actually waited until we had done so, therefore there was

Chapter 2: Superstitions

almost an expectation that customers would want to participate in this ritual. Even though I do not personally believe that an inanimate statue such as this one can bring good fortune, I complied and rubbed the statue's head because I felt obliged to. This example is a pertinent reminder that superstitious beliefs can be started about any animal or object if you have a large enough following to make the idea believable.

The Guardian Newspaper printed a very interesting article last year which revealed that just two of the UK's 14 best restaurants have a table 13, with most simply skipping from 12 to 14. The article expands on the very notion that the number 13 is considered unlucky. *"According to Jason Atherton, a graduate of Spain's famous El Bulli and head chef at Pollen Street Social, not having a table 13 'is something that has always happened in restaurants'".* Emmanuel Landré, general manager of the Le Gavroche restaurant, says that customers are as apprehensive as proprietors. When people book up the whole restaurant and devise their own seating plans, *"99% of the time they avoid number 13 on purpose. It may be irrational but a curse is a curse and nobody wants a curse.* Picking up on Chinese traditions, he also notes that *"if the number eight is somewhere in the business – either in the address or the telephone number – it's a good sign,"* which is just as well since you'll find his restaurant at 8-10 Pollen Street. The number 8 is considered lucky in Chinese culture because the pronunciation of the word is "ba" which sounds very similar to the word for prosperity which is "fa". Also, the number has a perfectly symmetrical shape which is believed to lead to perfect balance – the ideal in Chinese Astrology. This number has such special significance that the Olympic Games in China started on 08.08.08 and a record number of weddings were recorded on that day.

The article continues by stating that, in many ways, it is fitting that the restaurant world should be so full of superstitions because one of the oldest forms of triskaidekaphobia (fear of the number 13) is the idea that if 13 people gather at a table, one will be dead within a year. Although the true source of this superstition is unclear, the origins may be found in two stories involving dining. First, there is the Last Supper, where Jesus ate with his 12 disciples and the 13th man in the room betrayed him. Also, there is the Norse legend of the 12 gods invited to a banquet in Valhalla which was then gatecrashed by Loki, the spirit of strife and mystery, and as a consequence, Balder, the favourite of the Gods, was killed. However, one must bear in mind that, as the Radfords wrote in their 1949 Encyclopaedia of Superstitions *"This would hardly account for the dislike of the Romans and Greeks for the number 13"*

Interestingly, the Leonardo Di Vinci painting of the last supper depicts the night before Jesus was betrayed. If you study the picture closely you will discover that a salt holder has been knocked over (right beside Jesus) allegedly by Judas which could have been the start of the superstition that such an action brings about bad luck. The superstition holds that the devil lurks behind you so you must throw salt over your left shoulder so that it gets the devil in his eye.

It's quite astonishing to think that even the most popular and expensive restaurants subscribe to superstitious beliefs. You would think that the further up the social hierarchy you are, the more cynical you would be towards believing superstitious rituals, however the examples described here prove otherwise.

Lucky cat

Another interesting superstitious belief is the lucky cat ornament (or Maneki Neko – roughly translating as beckoning cat) that originated in Japan and features in many Chinese and Asian restaurants. In my local Chinese takeaway sits a lucky cat which has its left arm raised with Chinese script running down it. This means that the owners of the statue are hoping that he will bring good fortune to the business – it is as if the cat is beckoning customers to enter. If the cat was raising its right arm, this would bring good luck into people's homes. I had a chat with the takeaway owner who told me that in Chinese culture, the lucky cat is very symbolic and must be treated like a member of the family. She told me that she polishes the cat every day and she firmly believes that the success of her business is down to her lucky cat ornament. She also told me that she was bought this cat by a friend of hers as it is considered to be unlucky if you buy one for yourself. This is similar to the superstition already mentioned whereby it is unlucky to buy a purse for yourself.

The origin of the 'beckoning cat' belief is undecided, but one legend has it that a cat belonging to a very poor group of Chinese monks in a temple saved some rich Samurais from being struck by lightning by beckoning them with its paw away from the exact spot where the lightning was about to strike. As a reward, the Samurais bequeathed the Monks a large estate and when the cat died, a cat shrine was built in its memory and people made models of the cat with the waving paw in order to bring themselves good luck. Another story has it that a famous Japanese woman was about to be attacked by a dangerous snake but luckily her favourite cat realised what was about to happen and raised his paw to warn her, but was killed by the snake in the process. To honour the cat, she had an effigy of it carved into wood which then became popular with others as they were seen as offering protection from danger (Morris, 1999).

The colour of the beckoning cat is also significant, as described below:

White: happiness, purity and positive things to come

Human Behaviour

Black: beckon good health or ward off evil spirits

Green: good health

Calico: Traditional colour combination, considered to be the luckiest

Gold: Wealth and prosperity

Red: Success in love and relationships

Also, sometimes the cat is designed to be holding something to bring even more good luck, such as a fish or a marble/gem.

Aircraft superstitions

You may be surprised to learn that, according to a survey by seatguru.com, out of the

102 airlines they tracked, 25 around the world have no row 13 on their planes. Also, the flight numbers of crashed planes are never re-used, and there is never a flight 13. Before it merged with United Airlines, Continental airlines completely avoided the number 13 – there was no gate 13 at hub airports and no row 13 on their aircraft. It's not just the number 13 that can cause problems in the aviation industry – 666 can have a similar effect and is avoided as a flight number by many airlines. One which does not conform is Finnair, who, on a light-hearted note, regularly run a flight bearing this number from Copenhagen to Helsinki, meaning you can take flight 666 to HEL (the airport code for Helsinki).

Some people, upon entering an aircraft, will either touch or even kiss it in the belief that this will ensure they have a safe flight (as mentioned previously). Some people report taking a lucky charm or toy with them on the plane or will listen to the same song whilst flying.

A curious superstition is that upon unveiling a new air traffic control tower, a ceremonial cedar tree is placed on top. This is apparently a construction industry tradition that originated in Scandinavia and brings good luck upon the new building.

As you have read, the incredible belief that certain people have regarding superstitious rituals is growing. Human behaviour is filled with unexplained events, and the fact that superstitions now influence the areas of sport, restaurant dining and airline travel (together with the rising popularity of internet-based superstitious messages) shows that they are very much a part of everyday life, even in today's modern times. I must confess to you that this section has been the most fascinating area I have covered in the realms of human behaviour. I have written at length about my concerns at how technology is rapidly advancing, with bigger and more intelligent machines being invented, however some superstitious beliefs and rituals have outlasted the many changes the world has seen. The belief people place in a variety of charms, amulets, trinkets and lucky numbers is fascinating, and one which shapes their daily life. The aim of this section was not to present my findings to dispute the validity of certain superstitious rituals and beliefs (no matter how bizarre they may be) but to showcase to you that human behaviour can be influenced by many often surprising beliefs. Where superstitions end and compulsiveness starts is a matter which is open to much debate.

Chapter 3: Human body language

Introduction

As you have read, emotions and superstitions affect both body and mind. Emotions frequently trigger a response in the body which can only last only a few seconds, whereas certain superstitions can either be a part of your daily life, or only reveal themselves once in a blue moon. However body language is different, because it has always been a part of your life, whether you realise it or not. As I've mentioned at the start of my second book, body language is a truly powerful communicator, and has been since your childhood. You, the reader, have been part of a fascinating world around you, often totally oblivious both to the messages you're sending out to those around you and those being transmitted by your friends, family and strangers. Our words may deliver one message, but our body could reveal something contradictory. It's quite astonishing to think that roughly, over three quarters of what we convey to others is transmitted via our speech tones, gestures, movements, mannerisms, expressions and our uniquely acquired personal idiosyncrasies. Former FBI Spy catcher Joe Navarro expands on this on his website - "*It's estimated that as much as 80% of our interaction with others is through non-verbal communication, or body language. And the vast majority of the nonverbal cues we display are driven by our subconscious mind*".

Incidentally, I have covered the study of body language in my two previous books. My first was a fascinating look at Michael Jackson's body language during 5 TV interviews that he gave at different stages of his life, and the book offered a refreshing look at Michael's behaviour from a different perceptive. I believe I am the first author to publish a book solely dedicated to analysing the non-

Chapter 3: Human body language

verbal behaviour of an individual in this way. The international success of that book gave me the inspiration to discuss the principles of body language in my second book *'Unmasked: A Revealing Look At The Fascinating World Of Body Language'* where I educated the reader on many interesting topics, such as the vast cultural behavioural differences that exist from region to region, how to become more adept at reading facial expressions and how to become more skilled at improving your own body language to bring about success. I also covered in my final thoughts that I was unclear as to how the study of non-verbal communication will eventually end up. I gave my doubts regarding the longevity of the topic, as I fear that the 'rise of the machines' will eventually provide the consumer with enough entertainment that leaving the house to interact with others will no longer be a necessity.

Perhaps I was being too critical on our species, however the increasing demand for power-hungry technology in our homes will eventually place the final nail in the coffin for the power stations, as one day in the none-too-distant future they will be unable to meet demand. Then, when electrical power finally ceases on this planet, we may end up going back to a variation of the primitive way of life seen by our forebears. Either one way or another, whether society becomes more dormant, or the rise of technology results in crippling power outages, the fight to remain as we are now will be over. As I have previously mentioned, Channel 4 aired a fictional documentary called *'Blackout'* earlier this year (2013) which showcased just this very scenario.

Correctly reading facial emotions and identifying concealment

Whilst working in the health and fitness industry, the ability to read emotions has served me greatly. Not all emotions that appear on the face can be taken (quite literally) at face value. The problem with reading facial expressions of emotion is that we see a facial expression and expect it to have the same meaning each time. Sadly, this isn't the case, and again is another reason why reading body language can be fraught with difficulties. The examples below will expand upon this point.

We communicate so much information on our faces and it is often used to emphasise key points during our statements. These are known as 'speech emblems' and help to punctuate our words. Just because our face moves, it doesn't mean that we are experiencing an emotion. Our eyebrows are great communicators, often illustrating and emphasising our words when they are raised or lowered. They will instinctively rise when we question the credibility of someone's story or statement, but remember that the presence of a facial movement doesn't necessarily mean the presence of an emotion. Sometimes there doesn't need to be any other bodily movement other than just the face. *'There are thousands of facial expressions, each different from one another. Many of them have nothing to do with emotion. Many expressions are what we call conversational signals, which, like body-movement illustrators, emphasize speech or provide syntax (such as facial question marks or exclamation points). There are also a number of facial emblems: the one-eye closure wink, the raised eyebrows - droopy upper eyelid - horseshoe mouth shrug, the one-eyebrow-raised scepticism, to mention a few. There are facial manipulators, such as lip biting, lip sucking, lip wiping and cheek puffing. And then there are the emotional expressions, the true ones and the false'* (Ekman 1985: 127).

Think about how you would react when your friend (who is known for their tall stories) tells you a story about how she met David Beckham last night, despite the fact you saw him on the news in China. Your face would probably reveal your scepticism, because when our friends repeatedly tell 'stories', we often flash contempt as we feel morally superior that we don't have to resort to inventing such stories to be popular. You could identify that contempt was being flashed by others by looking for a one sided smirk-like expression that reveals to you "I've heard all this before and who do you think you are fooling?" Social etiquette dictates that we are often obliged to listen to the speaker's story without voicing our true feelings about its validity. Society would crumble if we all started to answer all questions honestly and truthfully so sometimes, to keep the peace and to maintain the status quo, we have to wear a mask which hides our true feelings.

During our interactions with others, our facial muscles are constantly contracting. However, not every expression you see on the face is an accurate representation of someone's current feelings. For example, if the above friend was telling you a joke which is taking forever to get to the punchline, the listener might hold their smile for longer than normal (in fact, sometimes, it ends up looking like a grimace). I often find myself doing this as I don't wish to offend the speaker, so instead I hold my expression so that it appears I'm excited to hear the punchline, when in fact I have heard the joke 100 times before. Here I am simulating the expression so that it appears that I'm interested when I'm not. I know full well that my expression doesn't fit the 'interested' look, but I'm also aware that most people are oblivious to the fact that I'm not actually experiencing the happiness I show. One way you can spot this is to notice how long the expression lasts for on the face. The smile is probably the easiest expression to falsify as many people are practised at concealing their emotions behind a smile. Also the smile is so well consciously remembered that it takes very little thought in order to contract a necessary smile. The same can't be said for the expression of sadness which can look very 'put on' when a person is consciously trying to express the facial emotion that they don't feel.

Quite often, people will attempt to conceal their emotions for various reasons, such as to keep up appearances or because they know that it would not be acceptable to display a certain emotion in the situation they find themselves in. For instance, if a person just watched a sad movie, it would be inappropriate to run out into the street crying hysterically. As already discussed, poker players have a solid reason for becoming well-versed at concealing their emotions because great sums of money can be at stake.

Naturally this concealment of emotion starts with the face because this is the place where most people look first. However if the emotion is strong, it may eventually leak out onto the face. When this happens, there is often an attempt to obscure the face from public view, which is done in a variety of ways. When a footballer misses an important penalty kick, they will often pull their shirt over their face or cover their face with their hands so that their grief is no longer visible to their supporters. Upset or reprimanded children will often hide their face into their bedroom quilts to avoid showing any facial emotion. I strongly believe that this is done to avoid showing the emotion because it could be perceived as a sign of weakness.

On the other end of the spectrum are those people who suffer from a mental health condition called depression. During the years I have spent working with clients with mental health conditions, I have had many an opportunity to speak to people who were battling with depression. In certain situations, their sadness has to be masked with another emotion. The problem with this is that certain anti-depressants can promote muscular atrophy of the face, resulting in the facial muscles (especially around the corners of the mouth) looking droopy. This automatically makes someone look sad even if they aren't currently feeling depressed. I have personally found that the masking of facial emotions (putting on an emotion that isn't felt) is the preferred method of managing facial expressions for those with depression, perhaps because they are afraid of others ridiculing their sadness. I have previously mentioned in the chapter on emotions that Dr. Ekman states that not everyone empathises with the sadness of others. Maybe one reason for masking their actual emotion is so that they look happy and therefore aren't likely to be ridiculed if their expression is a positive one.

So the obvious question is how do you spot an expression that has been put on and isn't actually felt? Has there ever been a more important question? Does your local car salesman really know that there isn't a problem with the car you're about to buy from him, and is that really the lowest price he'll accept for the car? If you have an understanding about how the face works, it will help you to identify when you are potentially being misled. I will now provide you with a few helpful hints to ascertain whether or not the expression you see is felt or simulated.

Timing and synchronisation of gestures and facial expressions

Timing and synchronisation can play important roles in detecting falsified expressions and emotions. Gestural timing is where there is complete harmony between an expression and a corresponding gesture to ensure that the message being sent is more likely to be perceived as honest. Imagine Lord Sugar (or Donald Trump) saying 'you're fired' then 3 seconds later pointing towards the unfortunate candidate on the popular TV show *The Apprentice*. This would look noticeably out of place and you would probably furrow your brow to reflect your puzzlement. Words and gestures need to be in sync in order for their desired meaning to be successfully interpreted by onlookers.

Of all emotional expressions, surprise is the briefest, but the problem with spotting this emotion in others is that it happens so fast that by the time you've blinked, it might have blended into another emotion (either happiness if for instance you are reacting to a surprise party or any other subsequent emotions such as fear or anger). Surprise is displayed so fast facially that if it lasts for more than a second it's probably a simulated emotion. If you knew before you walked through your front door that your friends and family were behind the door, your surprised expression would look put on. Which areas of the face contract, how long are they contracted for and what the immediate subsequent facial movement is are all areas that you need to consider when debating the validity of a facial expression.

Dr. Ekman's research has suggested that the lower part of the face might be a significant place to observe if you are looking for expressions of emotion that you believe to be simulated.

"Watch out for what people do in the lower part of the face, particularly the lips and the lines around the nose and lower cheek. Although we do not yet have evidence to prove this, our study of facial expressions suggests that when a person is controlling what is shown on his face, more effort is focused on managing what occurs in and around his mouth and lips than in the area of the eyes/lids or brows/forehead" (Ekman, 2003: 158-159)

The mouth is the source of speech, so greater care is taken to control the muscle action around the jaw, because the mouth has a vital role to play in the expressing of many emotions, particularly those which are more extreme. Examples would include spitting to show disgust or screaming to show terror. The 7 basic emotions

Chapter 3: Human body language

that are universal to homosapians all have significant actions around the jaw (smile in happiness, smirk in contempt etc) so a simulated expression might have less action in the lower face as this is the area used most frequently when we are displaying a genuinely-felt emotion.

Interestingly, I have recently watched a documentary series called *First Dates* on Channel 4 which offered a close-up look at modern dating, and it contained some great examples of how the face responds to certain situations. I must make a point here, namely that I am unsure if the behaviour on show is real and not simulated as one can never be sure of the true validity of certain television programmes. I made this point in my first book when I outlined that when we feel we are being watched, we are never our true selves, as due to the presence of the cameras, we would not behave in a manner that is considered 'normal' for us (Baxter, 2012: 160).

During one particular episode, upon their first meeting, a lady's date instigated a hug, which provoked a flash of disgust from her whilst in the embrace. Maybe she was hoping for someone better looking, or maybe he had a smell about him that she did not like. In this example, we do not know what caused this lady to flash this expression, and Ekman further emphasises this point when he says *"it is important to remember that emotional signals do not tell us their source. We may know someone is angry without knowing exactly why. It could be anger at us, anger directed inwardly at his or herself or anger about something the person just remembered that has nothing to do with us"* (2003: 74)

This example also demonstrates that our true hidden feelings can momentarily 'leak' out via our facial micro expressions (which you need to be trained to read otherwise you would miss them due to the speed at which they can occur). This expression of disgust by the lady mentioned above lasted less than a second and was followed by an attempt on her behalf to avoid eye contact. This was probably performed because prolonged eye contact can be a sign of attraction during a first date, and she didn't want to give him that idea during the first impression stage. A feeling of disgust is a feeling of aversion and the scrunching up of the face is done to prevent offending smells from travelling up the nostrils. Avoiding direct eye contact is done so that we don't make visual contact with whatever has made us feel disgusted. The chap in question certainly wasn't in my opinion physically disgusting, however his greeting of 'alright beautiful' and an obvious leer towards her chest more than likely provoked her disgust reaction. He was oblivious to this, as during the initial moments of a first date, it's often not polite to overly concentrate on the face of someone you've only just met.

Watching this programme is a great way to learn how expressions are managed on the face. Often when someone is concealing how they really feel, they will be less animated in their face. This corresponds nicely to the research that's been conducted in the field of emotional recognition which has shown that the more restricted the facial muscles are, the less emotion they convey. The very essence of learning to understand human body language is so you can use your newfound skills not only on your friends, but also to influence the behaviour of others who you may only just have met. Below, I will describe 5 key areas of body language that you are most likely to encounter during your daily interactions with others.

5 Essential Body Language Terms

Number 1 is Emblems, which describes gestures when they are used as a substitute for words, much like the role sign language plays in everyday life. Emblems have a very precise meaning and replace a verbal message as no words are needed to interpret and comprehend the message (for a visual aid regarding this gesture,

Chapter 3: Human body language

think of a policeman silently stopping traffic in the street with his arm raised and palm facing outwards). Other examples of emblematic gestures would be giving the thumbs up sign when something is good, or waving goodbye to someone who is leaving. Emblems are culturally specific so their meaning may differ depending on where in the world you are. For example, the 'okay' sign made with the thumb and index finger means everything is 'okay' in the UK and the USA, however the same sign means money in Japan, and in Turkey it carries an offensive message because it is seen to resemble a certain bodily orifice. Ekman states that *"emblems have a very precise meaning, known to everyone within a cultural group. Most emblems are performed right out in front of the person, between the waist and the neck area. An emblem can't be missed when it is in the presentation position."* (1985, 103)

Number 2 is Illustrators, which are sometimes referred to as 'iconic' gestures. These are movements that accompany speech to illustrate something, like the size or shape of an item. When we nod our heads to emphasise a point during a conversation, this would be an example of an illustrator. The hands are not the only way that an illustrator can be expressed, as I mentioned the role of the eyebrows earlier when discussing speech emblems. Ekman further emphasises this point when he states:

"Illustrators are called by that name because they illustrate speech as it is spoken. There are many ways to do so: emphasis can be given to a word or phrase, much like an accent mark or underlining; the flow of thought can be traced in the air, as if the speaker is conducting her speech; the hands can draw a picture in a space or show an action repeating or amplifying what is being said. It is the hands that usually illustrate speech, although brow and upper eyelid movements often provide emphasis illustrators, and the entire body or upper trunk can do so also" (Ekman, 1985, 104-105)

Human Behaviour

Number 3 is Regulators, which are movements that signal a conversational change between two or more people - for example, when one person has just finished speaking, they may lower their arms/hands to allow the next person to speak. This is the particularly dominant body language seen in Italy, where people jostle for the lead position during a conversation. We also nod our heads to signify whose turn it is to speak, and the eye glare can be used to signal to someone that it would be inappropriate to speak. An example of this would be if a mum and her son and daughter were sat in a room together and the son began asking his mother if she'd like a particular type of perfume for Christmas, not realising that his sister has already bought her the exact same one. In this example, the sister may make repeated eye glares towards her brother to try to give him the hint that he is to change his mind about buying that particular type of perfume. Regulators can be especially prominent during a business meeting and are often performed by the boss who may nod or use their eye gaze to silently signal whose turn it is to speak next and offer their input.

Number 4 is Manipulators. These are signs of nervousness, or possible habit. Examples of this are playing with objects, scratching the head and rubbing the neck. One of the great body language myths is that liars show these types of nervous behaviours, however modern day research shows that this isn't always the case. Manipulators do not help the receiver understand the verbal or non-verbal message, and can often actually hinder the message being sent. *"Manipulators include all those movements in which one part of the body grooms, massages, rubs, holds, pinches, picks, scratches, or otherwise manipulates another body part. Manipulators may be of very short duration or they may go on for many minutes. Some of the brief ones appear to have a purpose: the hair is rearranged, matter is removed from the ear canal, a part of the body is scratched. Other manipulators, particularly those that last a long* *time, seem to be purposeless: hair is twisted and untwisted, fingers rubbed, a foot tapped."* (Ekman, 1985: 109-110)

Finally, **Number 5** is Affect Displays. These are sometimes known as 'emotional expressions' and these displays give us an indication of a person's emotional state. Chapter 1 elaborates upon the whole area of emotions in far more detail. Our facial expressions show the world how we feel, and the interpretation of character and temperament based on facial expressions is known as 'physiognomy'. The way we walk (gait) can be another example of an affect display, as this also sends out to others a silent message regarding our current emotional state. The way a person walks can vary from them having a 'spring in their step' to walking in a slow methodical way with their head down, and each of these would portray a different mood to onlookers.

The Power of Body Language

How to display confidence to others

Using body language to your advantage is a technique which can really work in your favour, both in your personal and work life. Below I am going to cover three body language actions which will enable you to convey a confident-looking display to others.

Steepling gesture

The first gesture is called the steeple or steepling gesture, which occurs when the fingers are pressed towards the sky in an almost church-like steeple or prayer position. This gesture can be used when you believe you have the right answers, as it is interpreted as a sign of confidence. However, too much steepling, and at the wrong time (timing and synchronisation) can make you appear smug and pompous – both undesirable traits, especially in the workplace. The steeple can be made towards the sky, or can be pointed towards someone, but the latter is more associated with being direct and aggressive. The steepling gesture is often used to display our confidence or to enlighten, however, overuse of this gesture can send out an egotistical message by stating non-verbally 'I am superior" to the receiver. Politicians will have body language coaches (much like myself) to guide them into making the right impression, and so they can learn how to get their point across to the voters to make them look like they can deliver on their promises without appearing too self-satisfied.

Palms down

The second action is keeping your palms down when you want people to listen. If you need to get your point across at work, consciously rotate your palms down when you're speaking. Keeping the palms open whilst making an emphatic statement counteracts the point you're making and can inadvertently reveal pleading. If you need to make a declarative statement and want to really emphasise your point, keep those palms down for greater success. As Morris describes, the palm down is the restraining hand of the cool headed, and hand batons like this reveal an urge to damp down or lower the prevalent mood or to control it by reduction (2002: 82).

Power stance

If you're ever in need of a confident-looking display, widen your stance as you're talking, because this will make you look bigger and more confident. If you use the palms-down gesture just mentioned together with a widened stance, your message will be delivered with much more authority and you will be more convincing. Posture plays an integral role in how others perceive you and is especially important when delivering key messages to a large audience.

Chapter 3: Human body language

Postural change is important as first impressions are vital, and someone with a slouched figure will send out a negative impression, and it will be hard to engage in a positive transaction because of this. We can interpret a number of different perceptions about someone based on reading their posture; we can potentially understand a person's state of mind, from being depressed, submissive or shy. We can also see if that person is feeling positive or negative about any given situation by watching for tell-tale body language signs. For instance, if during a presentation, a person was using a lot of blocking behaviours such as arms folded across the chest or was making repeated speech errors or hesitations, these would be signs that the person is lacking in confidence or had prepared poorly. In contrast, if the speaker was making use of many of the confident gestures described in this section, then that would portray their poise, self-assurance and power.

Body language and game playing

A game some people play to make you believe they have a connection with you is called Gestural Echoing. This is when one person uses a specific gesture, and another person will use that same gesture moments later (either subconsciously/inadvertently or deliberately). Gestural Echoing is a form of mirroring used to build or maintain a rapport with someone, and can have different intentions. It can be used to maintain long-lasting friendships (where two old friends do not consciously realise they are mirroring each others' exact stances) or conversely it could for instance be used by a car salesman who deliberately matches your body language and gestures to make you believe that they have a connection with you and understand your needs. Further examples of the tricks that car salesmen use can be found in Dr Britt's 2013 book as mentioned in chapter 1.

Personality and mood have a marked effect on the number of gestures we employ. The more positive gestures we send out, the more of a happy person we appear. Gestures and emotions are linked together, so we can decode gestures to work out the personality of that individual. It is interesting to note that open body movements and gestures are very useful when trying to persuade or convince a person to change their mind about something, or when trying to alter a person's perspective on something. We use persuasive words to help us to convince someone that our idea is potentially better than theirs, however with body language being a powerful communicator, open body movements should not be overlooked when attempting to change a person's mind.physiognomy (interpretation of character and temprement based on her current facial expression physiognomy (interpretation of character and temprement based on her current facial expression physiognomy (interpretation of character and temprement based on her current facial expression dddddddddddddddddddddddddd

Body language of a liar

I have decided to include this section because there is much debate (and many common myths and misconceptions) about what body language a liar does show. Most articles on body language start with information on how to spot lying and deception; however I feel that addressing the myths first will help to combat the rise in their popularity. The most common myth is that liars look away from you (avert their gaze) when they are lying. This is a false belief which can be backed up with 40 years of research (see bibliography for the link). What you will find is that a liar will often consciously engage in **greater** eye contact, because it is commonly (but mistakenly) believed that direct eye contact is a sign of truthfulness.

Chapter 3: Human body language

Some eye gaze behaviour is well rehearsed, such as when women use their gaze to attract males and persuade them into taking a course of action they might not otherwise have taken. Another reason is that eye gaze is related to many factors that have nothing to do with deception. People make less eye contact when they are embarrassed and make more eye contact when dealing with people of a high status rather than a lower one. Additionally, people avoid eye contact with those who sit too close to them and invade our personal space, and, as mentioned, some women use eye gaze to emotionally manipulate (Vrij, 2008). For these reasons, no relationship exists between eye gaze and deception.

Another classic myth which has made its way into prominence is using eye direction to detect deceit. I conducted research on this belief and found that the vast majority of people I questioned had heard about the 'eye movement linked to deception' myth and worryingly, most people believed that looking in a certain direction was a reliable sign of deception. Resent research conducted in 2012 has significantly disproved this theory and the link to the full article can be found in the bibliography.

Detecting deception via body language alone is fraught with difficulties. Research has suggested that truth-tellers can often appear more nervous than a liar, which is a result of the emotion 'fear'. The panic a truth-teller feels when they see their story is not being believed will arouse fear, which in turn will manifest into nervous energy and look suspicious to an unskilled lie-catcher. Some skilled liars may successfully control their deceptive behaviour and speech which removes the chance to observe such cues. Also, it is interesting to note that increased cognitive load (required when liars are formulating a false story in their head as they speak) has been shown to suppress behavioural animation. Liars want to make an honest impression on you and can attempt to control their deceptive behaviour accordingly. Truth-tellers are not as wary of their behaviour and can look more uncomfortable when challenged.

'Detecting a lie is not always easy. Lies are often embedded in truths and behavioural differences between people who are lying and people who are telling the truth are usually very small. In addition, some people are just really good at lying. Lie detection professionals routinely make common mistakes, including overemphasizing nonverbal cues, neglecting intrapersonal variations (i.e. how a person acts when they are telling the truth versus when they are lying), and being overly confident in their lie-detection skills'. (Vrij, Granhag, Porter, 2011)

However, despite the many popular myths associated with lying, research has indicated that the use of a higher pitch of voice, a slower speech rate, a decrease in illustrator hand gestures or hand/arm movements, fake smiles, head movements (persuasive), non-immediate answers and a lack of plausibility are reliable signs of deceit, so long as they appear in a cluster and not singularly. But please note, there is no single clue akin to Pinocchio's nose in detecting deceit, so therefore no single guaranteed sign of deception. However for greater accuracy, the lie spotter should focus their attention on the words of the liar, as these are the carriers of the deceit. Analysing the statements of the liar is more effective than looking for non-verbal signs of deceit for two main reasons. Firstly, the lie-catcher may have an incorrect belief about what behaviour the 'typical' liar shows, or secondly they may be unable to accurately interpret the non-verbal behaviour on show (falsely believing it to reflect the person's guilt). Either one of these errors may potentially render an innocent person guilty, and such mistakes have been termed as the Othello Error (see the entry in the body language terminology section in Appendix 2 for a further explanation).

Chapter 3: Human body language

'Despite its usefulness, there are several reasons why I feel an interviewer should not focus on a person's nonverbal gestures. If your attention is drawn to the interviewee's body movements, then you probably are not listening to everything the person is saying. This is important because people's words will betray them. It may only be one or two words that will let you know this person is being deceptive. If you focus on their hands, feet and eyes, then you may miss these few words that reveal his true thoughts.' (McClish – for link, see bibliography)

After this quote I feel it is important to point out that I am not saying that if you wish to catch a liar, then you must totally ignore the person's body language and focus solely on their words – that may result in you failing to spot a body language 'tell' that betrayed the fact that they were not being truthful with you. Such 'tells' could include those already mentioned together with an increase in speech fillers where the speaker is making a lot of pauses in their speech which are filled with 'ums' or 'erms'. These give the liar more valuable time to fabricate the story in their head or decide which information to omit. There may also be an increase in speech errors, so the speaker may repeat what they've already said, leave some of their sentences unfinished or make revealing "slips of the tongue".

Greeting displays

An area of non-verbal communication which is frequently overlooked is how we greet our friends, family and complete strangers. Often our greetings are performed without thought or hesitation, however to onlookers they provide valuable clues to our relationship with that person.

As Morris (2002) highlights, our greeting displays are determined by the following 5 areas:

1. The nature of the relationship with that person. We greet

strangers, friends, love interests and our spouses differently.

2. The duration of the separation. We often greet friends we haven't seen for years differently than those we saw last week.

3. Where the greeting takes place. Some people are uncomfortable with public displays of affection, no matter how long the separation. However this effect changes when the greeting is performed in private.

4. Which greetings are culturally acceptable in that country. Research the customs and etiquettes of the country you are visiting to avoid making the wrong impression on a stranger. For example, giving everyone you meet in Japan a deep bow is considered offensive even though your intention was to be courteous, as this gesture is reserved for greeting people who are of significant importance.

5. If there has been a change since the last meeting. Good news such as a marriage, birth, promotion or award will affect your next greeting with that person in the same context. You will also greet someone differently if they had suffered a bereavement or other bad news since your last meeting.

Body language gestures and their meanings

Giving the middle finger is a widespread insulting gesture seen throughout the world, as it carries the same meaning no matter where you are. It is one of the oldest documented obscenities and one of the most offensive. According to history, Ancient Roman Emperor Caligula was said to have forced his loyal subjects to kiss his extended middle finger instead of his hand. However this show of contempt eventually cost Caligula his life, as one of his citizens, Cassius, assassinated him.

The V-sign finger gesture (when shown with the back of the person's hand facing the receiver) is an almost uniquely British insult. It does have a historical explanation, because apparently, during the Norman invasion, English archers were told that if they were to lose their battle, they would have their bow-fingers severed (index & middle), thus rendering them useless as an archer. This punishment would obviously be detrimental to the soldier, and it would serve as a constant reminder of his failure. The successful archer in contrast would show his bow-fingers to the enemy to goad them, and in addition it would act as a reminder to rivals of his triumph and prowess as an archer.

The tongue protrude is an inborn action that has been hardwired into our brains since birth. As infants, when we'd had enough to eat, we would manoeuvre our head away from the source, whether it be a spoon, breast or bottle, so some might argue that the 'No' headshake actually originates from our instinctive response to reject food that we don't need. A study quoted in Morris (2002) showed that instead of showing concentration, the protruding tongue gesture actually signifies 'Please don't talk to me', because speech is impossible if the tongue is protruding out of the mouth. The study has shown that nursery school children protruded their tongues when they wanted to avoid any social contact with other children. Some adults still use the tongue display when performing a difficult task, and it is worth remembering that it is not a good idea to talk to someone displaying such a gesture, as they are showing you non-verbally that they are not interested in talking.

To 'doff the hat' is a courteous gesture seen throughout the world, and is often a subconscious greeting shown to those who are superior to us. Removing the hat originates from a welcoming gesture performed centuries ago, where most hats covered the face, so it was considered impolite to conceal one's face to a person of a higher status. Removing the hat also decreases our size, making us appear smaller, which aids in the body lowering process (bowing) performed to those of a higher social status than us. Research has also shown that the inside of the hat must not be shown as the garment could be dirty, which would be a great insult and a sign of disrespect to a person of significant importance.

Bowing is a worldwide sign of respect given to those who have a greater authority than us, with the depth of the bow being decided upon by the social status of the receiver. A small bow would be used to greet someone of a lower social grading, whereas a deep bow would be used when greeting someone who is significantly more important than oneself. The problem arises when holidaymakers visit countries like Japan, China, Korea, Taiwan or Vietnam and inadvertently give deep bows to everyone they greet. This is generally considered ignorant by the receiver, even though your intention was to be courteous to the customs of that country.

The standing leg cross is used when we don't feel threatened by our conversation partner, or when we feel safe in our current environment. In this position, you balance your body weight on one leg, making you physically unstable, which makes you vulnerable to attack should an aggressive situation arise. If you see this leg behaviour between two people, they have developed a good silent rapport with each other. I guarantee you won't stand like this with someone you feel threatened by, as your brain won't allow it.

The art of correctly reading and decoding body language is a skill which would benefit anyone who takes the subject seriously. Sadly, the scientific side of body language study is often dismissed as a pseudoscience, however as you will have read, gestures often have a very precise meaning which aids the communicative process. We are constantly communicating with others, and it's often our body language which sends out the most reliable messages regarding our true thoughts and feelings. I have highlighted how you can alter your own body language to bring about success or to enable you to take control of a situation. However, this does have its flaws, namely that if you're simply faking your displays, the timing and synchronisation between your words and gestures may look decidedly odd and very put-on. This will send out the wrong message to onlookers who are likely to think you are acting, so consciously altering your normal body language to achieve a desired outcome must be done carefully. As you will have read, our interactions with others can be heavily dependent upon successfully reading their verbal and non-verbal displays.

Final thoughts

As you have read, emotions and human body language play an integral role in everyday life, however it is the constant rise and popularity of modern day superstitious beliefs which have a really surprising role to play. At the very beginning of this book, long before any serious research took place, I had my doubts as the validity of superstitious beliefs and how many people would still actually believe in them in this day and age. I felt that I would be met with a certain degree of cynicism, however I was astonished to realise that certain beliefs all have a real bearing on people's lives. These superstitions can stem from a childhood belief or because they've been passed down from grandparents or because they appear in popular culture. Emotions and body language are a part of us all, however superstitious beliefs in my opinion are increasing in both form and popularity. As I have previously mentioned, it is the rise of social media, emailing and text messaging that has enabled superstitions to infiltrate our lives in new ways, provoking an emotional response in the process. Superstitions have also found their way into the sporting world as described, and there is an ongoing debate regarding where a superstition ends and a compulsion begins. Plus, there is the argument that the performance of the rituals becomes a self-fulfilling prophecy.

Emotions are set in stone. Their response can be triggered both consciously and unconsciously, depending on a variety of factors. They affect everyone in the same way physiologically, however once the emotion has passed, it is often up to our conscious mind to decide what to do next.

Human body language is a remarkable subject which has been tainted for many years by the multitude of popular myths

Final thoughts

surrounding it. I have been studying non-verbal communication for many years and it is still unsettling when people inform me that body language is nothing more than a pseudoscience; a subject with no merit. It is a shame that many still consider the art of correctly deciphering body language as a whimsical pursuit. The research that has been conducted over the last 60 years by the likes of professionals such as Dr. Desmond Morris and Dr. Paul Ekman among many others has revolutionised how we look at our fellow humans. As Dr. Morris correctly states, we stick to a remarkable set of personal bodily actions which are as unique to us as our fingerprints. *'Despite the many fascinating variations that exist from region to region and society to society, every one of the thousands of millions of human beings alive today shares an almost identical genetic inheritance'* (Morris 1994:4) This means that the basic behaviours we see in other people are instantly recognisable. Granted there are vast cultural differences in terms of certain hand signals, postures and adornments which separate our behaviours, but we are all basically the same animal. The study of body language needn't be tarnished by mistruths. Look around you, as there is a wealth of information being sent by others from a variety of channels (postures, gestures, expressions, movements) that give you an inclination as to how that person is feeling and what they are intending to do next.

So what does the future hold for each of the three topics?

Emotions will forever be a part of our life, and how accurately we are able to recognise emotions in other people will in my opinion continue to improve. Micro-expression recognition training is a rapidly expanding market, with the aforementioned coffee machine being able to scan a face to recognise a yawn. It will only be a matter of time before technology is introduced that enables a company to hire a machine that can read a person's face to detect any possible deception leakage during a job or police interview.

This technology could then be taken one step further, as for instance, someone may be trying to get a job as a baggage handler in an airport in order to sneak something untoward onto a plane (such as drugs or an explosive device), and the machine could spot the reliable signs of concealment in the face. People will no longer need to be trained to spot micro-expressions and the footage from the machine can be re-watched as many times as needed to spot those who appear to be hiding something. Granted the machines will only be as good as their software, but with some quality information and research available in the present day, it's an exciting prospect to see what new technology will be developed in this area over the next 15-30 years.

Superstitions show no sign of relenting. The fear some people experience when they don't perform a superstition will keep them performing the act. The 'I'll do this just in case' philosophy is still as strong today as it was 100+ years ago. Incredibly, people are both reluctant to research why such a superstition exists and even more reluctant to let go of their chosen belief. Advancements in technology and the advent of search engines such as Google have made things easier for people to research anything they deem worthy of their curiosity, however this rise in technology has only fuelled the flames of superstitious beliefs. The rise in examples such as 'share this post or receive bad luck' or 'send this text to 13 friends or be cursed for a year' has enabled fear to be felt from every possible media outlet. My research has concluded that most people would much prefer to keep their personal superstitions quiet, as they often fear being ridiculed by friends or family for believing that certain actions, trinkets and amulets can ward off evil and prevent bad luck. It wouldn't surprise me if, to avoid losing their social status, those who told me that they didn't believe in a superstition actually secretly do. Those who don't believe often look down on those who do as a sign of weakness, because they have to go to extreme measures (such as believing in myths) to help prevent them from perceived 'bad luck'.

The study of body language will continue to grow. Much has been written on non-verbal communication, with young authors such as Stu Dunn, Eric Goulard and Sachchidanand Swami providing excellent further contributions to this subject. All communication is behaviour, and I firmly believe that everyone has an inbuilt need to better communicate with others. Body language will always have its place in history, but as I mentioned in *Unmasked,* perhaps the study of body language will become a lost art. Perhaps we will as a species become more and more reliant on using a computer or tablet to communicate with our friends and families. The reduction of face to face interaction might enable us to be more confident behind the screen, but when we meet in the flesh, we may be at a loss as to what certain gestures and expressions mean. Could this be a plausible possibility? Power outages caused by the expansion of technology or actual human contact lessening due to advancements in technology are both very real and frightening scenarios. It's quite worrying to me, as an author, that in order to complete this book, I relied on social media more than ever before due to its convenience and ability to reach people quickly from all over the world. The quick 'hi how are you?' instant message option was available at my fingertips rather than having to drive down the road to see my friends for a face to face chat. Either way, the future of emotions, superstitions and body language is quite literally in your hands. How your children, and your children's children will see the future world remains to be seen.

At the back of my first book *'Behind The Mask'* I added a section on body language terminology. This section was very well received in the subsequent reviews on Amazon, so I am including this amended section in Appendix 2 to help you understand certain key body language terms.

I would like to end this book with some final words. My uncle Colin sadly passed away during the writing of this book, and his funeral was a celebration of his life. The Minister who gave the service said something that will live long in my memory, and now hopefully in yours - that the real treasure in life is a loving family. We may strive for success at work, but when you're gone, your work accomplishments matter not. It's what you leave behind that is what's truly important - family. So dear reader, as you have finally reached the end of my book, remind yourself to do whatever makes you happy, because ultimately, that is what's truly important in life.

Love and best wishes,

Your friend

CJB

Appendix 1: Adrenaline-fuelled emotions

From an early age, I have always been fascinated with taking risks and the feelings you experience when risks are undertaken and safely negotiated. Some have described me as a thrill-seeker and others as a reckless idiot! I will describe to you two emotional experiences that I have experienced and I will discuss the emotions I felt during the overcoming of one of my greatest fears, heights.

Tandem Skydive – 25th July 2010

In the summer of 2010, I plucked up the extreme courage required to jump out of a perfectly good plane to undertake a tandem skydive in order to raise money for Help for Heroes. A few of my old enemies from school (who I'm still in touch with via Facebook) did offer to pack my parachute for me, but I politely declined. Skydiving has always been something I had wanted to do, but it was especially testing as I have always had a phobia about heights and I have never been a good flyer, so before the big day, my emotions were already heightened.

An interesting fact about my skydive is that I was doing it as a tandem, meaning that I was to be strapped to an experienced instructor as I jumped out. This added another dimension to this experience, because I had to place my total trust in this instructor – my life was completely in his hands. I felt nervous and anxious about doing this, but as a first-time skydiver, I had no other choice but to complete the jump as part of a tandem. This man was a total stranger and despite having no emotional attachment to him, I was forced to place the ultimate level of trust in him - my life. His decisions would decide whether or not we both made it onto terra firma and lived to tell the tale.

Human Behaviour

I spent the previous 5 months under extreme duress, trying to lose the necessary body weight for the jump. My crisp-eating addiction had a tight grip on me, but I had to knock this on the head. I weighed 18 stone prior to the diet and my appetite resembled that of a Russian shot putter training for the Olympics. After many bleak and dark days of eating nothing but rabbit food and breadsticks and exercising like a man possessed (no link to a superstition intended), the big day finally arrived. I drove to the airfield on my own that fateful morning, and interestingly enough, until that day, I hadn't actually realised that there are two 6 o'clocks in one day. I thought I would distract myself by putting on a CD (ironically Michael Jackson's Number 1s) but it didn't help. I had a feeling inside me that was beyond anything I had ever experienced before, somewhere between anticipation, fear and outright terror.

As I was driving along the rural, windy roads en route to the airfield, a rat decided that at that exact moment, it was unhappy being on the left hand side of the road and would prefer new lodgings on the right. As I sadly flattened the creature under my left tyre, I hoped it wasn't a bad omen for the day ahead. I consoled myself with the thought of the Man vs. Food style blowout that I could consume once I'd finished the jump – that would make up for months of low calorie, bland, tasteless food.

I arrived at the airfield in good time and met my fellow jumpers. I am glad it wasn't just me who was in the grips of emotional turmoil as I witnessed some very significant body language from my fellow soon-to-be skydivers. Fear turns the body inside out, resulting in either the freeze, flight or fight limbic response. The problem with the fear we were all feeling is that it's not going to go away until you've jumped out of that plane and landed safely. There were more subtle displays of fear and more displacement behaviours than you could count: barrier gestures (e.g arms folded across the chest to

Appendix 1: Adrenaline-fuelled emotions

give comfort), gestural retreats (e.g. stepping away from the announcing tannoy) and severe blood depletion from the face (as previously mentioned, whilst experiencing fear, blood is diverted from the face to other places such as the legs so that you could run away from any danger). And of course, I was experiencing all these myself and more besides. I was unable to control my own behaviour because I was experiencing extreme discomfort. We were all summoned into the training room for our pre-jump briefing. It was quite a surreal moment, because we were being taught essential safety information about the jump, but I couldn't give the trainer my full attention because my brain was processing too much information related to my mixed feelings. My mind was full of a thousand questions and slight doubts were beginning to creep in, such as 'Why am I doing this? Is it such a good idea? What if something goes wrong?" But by the time the training had ended, it felt like I hadn't taken any of the information on board. We got changed into our jump suits and made our way outside for some much-needed fresh air. I felt as though my larger than average legs could buckle beneath me at any moment, leaving me crumpled and a laughing stock on the floor.

Thankfully, at that moment, my sister, auntie and uncle arrived, which gave me a much-needed moral boost (after they had commented that I looked like a convict at Alcatraz with my shaved haircut and overly-tight jump suit that resembled a straight jacket!) After pacing around the café area for what seemed like an eternity, the dreaded moment came booming over the tannoy: "CHRIS BAXTER TO THE JUMP ZONE". I presumed the bumbling tannoy announcer meant me......

At that moment, my heart rate jumped, my mouth went instantly dry and fear took over my every move. However, if I wasn't already at maximum terror, I was soon going to be. I met my tandem instructor and as we walked towards the airstrip, I was filled with a strong sense of trepidation. To my utter horror, my gaze was diverted towards the sky where I could see that a fellow skydiver was in a shocking and dangerous situation. His parachute had malfunctioned and was he spinning wildly out of control hundreds of feet up in the air. I watched as this poor man hurtled rapidly towards the ground, eventually crash-landing in a graveyard. So now you can just imagine my emotions. After already being terrified, I have just watched somebody quite literally fall from the sky, almost certainly receiving massive injuries, or perhaps (tragically) even dying. Panic ensued, klaxons were wailing, and in the distance I could see people running out of their cars to come to the aid of the stricken diver, and whilst all this was happening, the plane I was to jump out of had just landed. I tentatively hopped into the plane, thinking about what I had just seen – I couldn't stop the scene from re-playing over and over in my mind. There was another tandem jumper who was sat opposite me in the plane. I was doing my best to conceal my true feelings with some attempted behavioural control, but he on the other hand was in the grips of a stronger emotion than I was experiencing (and displaying) which I didn't think was possible. The intensity of fear that he showed is something that I will never forget. As the plane took off, his facial expression was almost stuck in permanent anguish. There were no micro expressions, no attempt to conceal his fear - just a permanent expression of absolute terror. We were up in the air for what seemed like an eternity, especially given my rising sense of fear. I later learned this delay was because the Air Ambulance was dispatched to help the stricken skydiver and we were not authorised to jump whilst it was on the ground. My fear of flying was somewhat subdued by watching my fellow skydiver experience a deeper emotion than mine - it made me feel somewhat better. As we reached 15,000ft, the ground team radioed in that it was now safe to jump… and as if by magic, the doors of the plane opened. It was time. All my fears, thoughts and decision-making literally went out of that door.

My fellow terrified skydiver was due to jump before me, but when his instructor turned to him and said "let's go", his body froze and he just shook his head and said "I'm not going to do it". This was the first time that I can recall seeing the flash-freeze response close up, where someone is so terrified that they almost turn to stone. Obviously, witnessing what had just happened to the unfortunate skydiver will hardly have helped this nervous skydiver's emotional state, however I did manage to put my fears to one side as I did not want to back out at this stage and let down the charity which was to benefit from this jump.

Next, my instructor said to me "Are you ready?" and I took a deep breath in and replied "Yes, let's do it". We were already strapped to one another as we shuffled our way to the plane door. We dangled our feet outside of the plane as we were hovering at 15,000 feet….I remember him saying "3…2….1… go" and then we tumbled forwards out of the plane. Soon we were falling at approx 120mph and I experienced a view of the world as never before. I felt exhilarated and somewhat overwhelmed, as I was very aware that I was getting to experience something that few others do. The all-encompassing sense of fear that I had felt during the morning was decreasing. The free-fall lasted about 90 seconds, then the instructor deployed the parachute. Unfortunately for me, as I am a larger than average guy, the next stage of the skydive caused me a few problems. The suit which I had to wear was quite a snug fit to say the least, which wasn't really an issue until the instructor pulled the cord to activate the parachute. The combined weight of myself (15 stone), the instructor (approx 12 stone) and the parachute (approx 3 stone) meant that roughly 30 stone was immediately slowed down. The straps of the bodysuit that I was wearing became unbearably tight and created tension at the top of my thighs, close to my femoral artery. This resulted in a restricted blood flow to my legs which made them feel numb and no longer a part of my body. Panic set in because I was a) beginning to feel faint due to the lack of blood flow to my brain and b) I knew that if I couldn't move my legs, then I wouldn't be able to land safely as described in the earlier (somewhat hazy) safety briefing.

I managed to ask the instructor behind me if it was normal not to be able to feel my legs - he informed me that this was unusual and I think at this point he must have realised that I was having a few difficulties. I recall feeling a lot worse and also feeling an increasing sense of panic regarding the fact that I would be unable to land safely. To try to stop me from fainting, he kept asking me questions to try to maintain my level of consciousness. The next thing I remember is him telling me to lift my legs up because landing was imminent. I would like to say that upon landing, I had a feeling of pure, unadulterated joy. However, the reality was far from that. I landed in an ungainly and undignified heap due to my lifeless legs. The instructor had to ask me politely to modify my French as the air was blue, which matched perfectly the colour of my lips.

I remember lying almost motionless as blood was finally able to circulate freely to my extremities. The instructor's face was a picture as I lay wiggling my toes in an attempt to regain feeling. I believe most people would have been overwhelmed with happiness after completing the skydive... not me. I was more elated that I didn't end up folded like a giant accordion in front of hundreds of spectators. My instructor politely reminded me to 'get up' as other people were circulating in the air ready to land. I winced back to the training room, removed the jump suit and met my family amid jubilant celebrations. My sister made the deeply flattering remark that I looked like I had aged 10 years in 10 minutes.

As I congratulated others on their jump, I bumped into the chap who was in the same plane as me who didn't jump. He congratulated me on my courage and explained to me why he didn't jump. He said that the experience of seeing that skydiver in peril made him feel physically sick and he couldn't bring himself to jump. That is what fear does to a person - it takes over your decision-making in a heartbeat. Before I left, he told me that he will try again, but interestingly if you back out of the skydive, you don't get financially refunded.

I got changed into my normal clothes and made my way home, and then the intense emotion started. I was literally singing Michael Jackson's 'Thriller' at the top of my voice as I was driving down the M6 motorway. The fear had passed and I was now filled with emotions such as pride, elation and a total sense of incredulity that I managed to bring myself to go ahead with the skydive after being in the all-encompassing grip of fear. That is the beauty of emotions, as sometimes you can't bring yourself to do something (the failed skydiver) and sometimes you can feel the fear, but can override the emotion.

Also, I hope you appreciated the deliberate use of humour in this article, as I was attempting to trigger an emotional response in you, the reader. If you laughed, smiled or even just smirked at any point whilst reading it, I have been successful in my attempt.

For those who are interested, the stricken skydiver suffered massive injuries, but survived.

Hot Air Balloon adventure

Human Behaviour

2/9/2012

I am now going to describe to you the most emotional experience of my life, and it again involves the emotion of fear. Hopefully, by reading my account, you will gain an understanding of the many ways that fear can manifest in the body.

Two years had passed since my last adrenaline fuelled escapade, so Kat and I decided (thanks to my bargain Ebay purchase) to watch the sunset in a hot air balloon. Kat doesn't have a fear of heights, which was just peachy as I knew upon booking this trip that it would take some serious courage from me to get up there, as heights have been a long-standing fear of mine (not helped by my near-miss skydiving)! So the big day came, and we arrived safely at the launch area. Our pilot gave us a quick briefing before setting about to inflate the balloon into its starting position. At this point, I daren't tell Kat that I was having second thoughts as I was by far the biggest chap there and it would have looked a bit pathetic if a burly 6 footer like myself had backed out at this stage. As the pilot shouted for everyone to hop into the basket, I thought it would be a good idea for me to get in first so I could find safety in the middle of the basket, well away from the edge, however disaster struck… the tallest have to go nearest the edge of the basket because the burner is placed in the middle and the tallest would get their heads burnt. Kat and I got into the basket (which hadn't left the ground at this point) and the pilot indicated to his team below to unclip the basket from the ground.

At this point the basket started to rise off the ground and into the air we went. Oh. My. Goodness. As we reached just 50 feet I could feel my heart pounding in my chest, and I was still holding onto the side of the basket with as much force as a crocodile's mouth shutting - I was totally frozen with fear. As the balloon slowly

Appendix 1: Adrenaline-fuelled emotions

reached its 1500ft target I was so scared that I was unable to speak or move. My legs felt like lead blocks that had been super-glued to the bottom of the basket. This is because the most basic response to fear is freeze, flight or fight, and my body had frozen me to the spot in order to prevent me from falling out. To make matters worse, my dearly beloved asked me to 'shift out of the way' so she could get a better shot of the curvature of the earth. As I took one baby step behind me I stepped on a rogue bit of wicker that snapped under my foot. Kat said my face was whiter than a sheep in a snowstorm. The colour drains from people's faces during a frightening situation because the blood is diverted away to more vital organs such as the heart and lungs. As we soared majestically above the clouds, the pilot told us all that it was time for a photo. The camera was mounted on a huge steel rod and he asked us all to turn around and smile for the camera. Yep, you guessed it, I was facing the wrong way. I think shimmying around that basket was probably the hardest manoeuvre I have ever done. We were up in that balloon for an hour and half and to top it all, we crash-landed into a farmer's field 30 miles off course due to high winds. It was an incredible experience, one I will never forget, but one thing is for sure, I would never attempt such an adventure again without the help of some exceptionally strong sedatives or some assistance from Mr. Jack Daniels.

An interesting point to note is that I did not take with me any lucky charms or amulets on any of these adventures as I did not believe that an object of any sort would help me to conquer my grave fear.

Appendix 2 : Body Language Terminology

Arms akimbo – Arms placed by the side of the body, used to show that there are issues present.

Baseline behaviour – Understanding what is 'normal' for an individual in terms of their verbal and non-verbal behaviour.

Blocking gesture – Done to block out the cause of stress. Can be performed with the legs, arms, hands, eyelids or any object. When we feel threatened, our natural instinct is to create a barricade between ourselves and the cause of the stress.

Brokaw Hazard – when a person's idiosyncrasies are misinterpreted as a sign of guilt, as the observer is unfamiliar with the person's baseline body language.

Displacement behaviour - Very similar to manipulators, and are tiny scratches of the body or clothing adjustments that serve no functional purpose yet reveal inner conflict or frustration.

Distancing language – Language used to create distance from a statement. "I did not have sexual relations with that woman" is an example of distancing language.

Duping delight. – Where a person feels delighted at their level of acting because their deception hasn't aroused suspicion in their target. Can also be seen when a person's lies result in an innocent victim being wrongly punished.

Emblematic gesture – Emblems have a precise meaning, like the 'thumbs up' hand gesture. No words are necessary to comprehend the meaning of the gesture.

False starts – When a speaker makes numerous speech errors at the start of their statement – often associated with discussing difficult subjects or when a person is telling an untrue story that they haven't had time to rehearse.

Flashbulb eyes – Momentary widening of the eyes, often seen during surprise.

Gestural slip – Gestures that contradict what's being said. A half shoulder shrug during a statement could indicate that the person knows more than they are revealing.

Gestural timing – Movements that are in synchrony with our words.

Hands behind back – Has a variety of meanings depending on context. Can be used to show how proud we are of something, that we are uncomfortable, or to show our superiority.

Hand scissors – A chopping action performed when one wishes to 'chop' the negativity in half.

Illustrators - Help us to exemplify our speech as it is spoken – examples would include head nods, pointing and hand gesticulations

Limbic response – This is responsible for the freeze, flight or fight response seen in humans that are facing danger. It originates in the limbic system, which is a complex set of structures found on both sides of the thalamus in the brain and supports a variety of functions such as emotions, behaviour and motivation.

Manipulators – When one part of the body grooms, massages, rubs, holds, pinches, picks, scratches or otherwise manipulates another part of the body in order to dissipate stress or tension.

Mannerisms/Idiosyncrasies - A habitual gesture or way of speaking or behaving.

Micro-expressions - Very brief expressions, showing concealed emotions. Can be as brief as 1/15 to 1/25 of a second.

Postural retreat – when the body moves away from something it dislikes

Steepling – Touching the spread fingertips of both hands, in a gesture similar to praying hands. Can be used to showcase our confidence, yet overuse can make the person appear pompous.

Tightening of the lips – Can be shown out of frustration, concealment, anger or embarrassment.

Tongue biting – Done to stop oneself from saying something that one may regret later.

Tongue protruding– Can be prevalent during moments of deep concentration, or during social avoidance.

Torso Lean – Moving away from something we don't like. Can also be referred to as a gestural retreat.

Universal behaviours – Behaviours that are carry the same meaning worldwide, such as crying or a shoulder shrug.

Universal facial expressions - There are seven of these and they are recognised worldwide: Happiness, Sadness, Anger, Disgust, Fear, Surprise and Contempt

Bibliography

Baxter, Craig. 2012. *Behind The Mask: What Michael Jackson's Body Language Told The World.* CreateSpace: Independent Publishing Platform.

Baxter, Craig. 2013. *Unmasked: A Revealing Look At The Fascinating World Of Body Language.* CreateSpace: Independent Publishing Platform.

Britt, Michael. 2013. *They Saw You Coming: Psychological Techniques Dealers Use to Get You to Buy.* Boots & Eddy Productions, LLC

Carnegie, Dale. 1981. *How To Win Friends and Influence People.* New York: Simon and Schuster

Darwin, Charles. 1872. *The Expression of Emotion in Man and Animals.* New York: Appleton-Century Crofts.

DEPAULO, BELLA. 1988. NONVERBAL ASPECTS OF DECEPTION. JOURNAL OF NONVERBAL BEHAVIOR

DUNN, STU. 2013. TRUE LIES: A GUIDE TO READING FACES, INTERPRETING BODY LANGUAGE AND DETECTING DECEPTION IN THE REAL WORLD. CreateSpace: Independent Publishing Platform.

Ekman, Paul and Friesen, W. V. 1969. *The repertoire of non-verbal behaviour: Categories, origins, usage and coding.* Semiotica, 1, 49-98

Ekman, Paul. 1978. *Facial Action Coding System: Investigator's Guide.* Pala Alto, Calif: Consulting Psychologists Press.

Ekman, Paul. 1985. *Telling Lies: Clues to Deceit in the Marketplace, Politics and Marriages.* New York: W.W. Norton & Co.

Ekman, Paul. 2003. *Emotions Revealed: recognizing faces and feelings to improve communication and emotional life.* New York: Times Books.

Ekman, Paul. 2005. *What the Face Reveals: Basic and Applied Studies of Spontaneous Expression Using the Facial Action Coding System (FACS)* Oxford University Press.

Givens, David G. 2002. *The Nonverbal Dictionary of Gestures, Signs & Body Language Cues.* (http://www.center-for-nonverbal-studies.org/6101.html)

GORDON, **N.J.** *& FLEISHER,* W.L. 2006 (2nd ed). *Effective Interviewing and Interrogation Techniques.* Academic Press: Boston

Goulard, Eric. 2013. *Body Language Secrets Revealed: How Cognitive Science Can Help You Shape Your Interactions.* CreateSpace: Independent Publishing Platform.

Leiberman, David. 1998. *Never be lied to again* New York: St Martin's press.

MATSUMOTO, DAVID. 2007. CULTURE, CONTENT AND BEHAVIOUR. *JOURNAL OF PERSONALITY, 75 (6), 1285-1319*

MATSUMOTO, DAVID. 2011. EVALUATING TRUTHFULNESS AND DETECTING DECEPTION: NEW TOOLS TO AID INVESTIGATORS. *FBI LAW ENFORCEMENT BULLETIN.* http://davidmatsumoto.com/content/Evaluating%20Truthfulness%20and%20Detecting%20Deception.pdf

MCCLISH, MARK 2010. I KNOW YOU ARE LYING. USA: The Marpa Group

McClish, Mark. 2013. Statement analysis online training. Available at www.statementanalysis.com/onlinetraining/ and

http://www.statementanalysis.com/nonverbs/ 2013)

Memon, Amina; Vrij, Aldert; Bull, Ray 2003. *Psychology and Law,*

Truthfulness, Accuracy and Credibility. London: McGraw-Hill

Morris, Desmond. 1985. *Bodywatching: a field guide to the human species.* London: Jonathan Cape

Morris, Desmond. 1994. *BodyTalk: A world guide to gestures.* London: Jonathan Cape

Morris, Desmond. 1994. *The Human Animal.* London: BCA

Morris, Desmond. 1999. *Body Guards: protective amulets and charms.* London: Element books

Morris, Desmond. 2002. *Peoplewatching: The Desmond Morris Guide to Body Language.* London: Vintage Books

Morris, Desmond. 2006. *The Nature of Happiness.* London: Little Books Limited

Morris, Desmond. 2009. *The Naked Man.* London: Jonathan Cape

Navarro, Joe. 2008. *What Every Body Is Saying.* New York: Harper Collins

Navarro, Joe. 2010. *Louder Than Words: Take Your Career from Average to Exceptional with the Hidden Power of Nonverbal Intelligence.* USA: Harper Collins

PEASE, ALLAN. *1981.* BODY LANGUAGE: HOW TO READ OTHERS' THOUGHTS BY THEIR GESTURES. *LONDON: SHELDON PRESS*

RADFORD, EDWIN, RADFORD, EDWIN.** 2010. **ENCYCLOPEDIA OF SUPERSTITIONS 1949. Kessinger Publishing

SWANTON, WILL. 2013. THE SLAMS. *AUSTRALIA: RANDOM HOUSE*

VRIJ, ALDERT. *2008.* DETECTING LIES AND DECEIT: *Pitfalls and Opportunities.* England: Wiley & Sons.

VRIJ ALDERT, GRANHAG, PAR ANDERS, PORTER, STEPHEN. 2011. PITFALLS AND OPPORTUNITIES IN NONVERBAL AND VERBAL LIE DETECTION (ARTICLE)

VRIJ, ALDERT; SEMIN, G. R., & BULL, R. 1996. *Insight in behaviour displayed during deception*. Human Communication Research.

Vrij, Aldert; Mann, Samantha; Fisher, Ronald; Leal, Sharon; Milne, Rebecca and Bull, Ray. 2007. Increasing Cognitive Load to facilitate Lie Detection: The benefit of recalling an event in reverse order.

Wiseman R, Watt C, ten Brinke L, Porter S, Couper S-L, et al. (2012) The Eyes Don't Have It: Lie Detection and Neuro-Linguistic Programming. PLoS ONE 7(7): e40259. doi:10.1371/journal.pone.0040259

See http://www.plosone.org/article/info%3Adoi%2F10.1371%2Fjournal.pone.0040259 for the research article.

Webb, David. 2012. *Criminal Profiling (The Essential Guide To Criminal Profiling)* Kindle edition.

Webb, David. 2013. *Inside The Criminal Mind: Behavioral Science Insights From The FBI*. Kindle Edition

Webb, David. 2013. The Incredibly Interesting Psychology Book. CreateSpace: Independent Publishing Platform

Webster, Richard. 2008. *The encyclopaedia of superstitions*. Llewellyn: USA

Wezowski, Kasia, Wezowski, Patryk. 2012. *The Micro Expressions*

Book for Business: How to read facial expressions for more effective negotiations, sales and recruitment. http://www.MicroExpressionsBook.com

Winston, Robert. 2005. *Body: An amazing tour of human anatomy.* London: Dorling Kindersley

Websites for further reading

http://www.all-about-body-language.com

http://www.all-about-psychology.com/

http://www.all-about-forensic-psychology.com/

http://www.all-about-forensic-science.com/

http://www.humintell.com

http://www.paulekman.com

http://www.british-sign.co.uk

http://www.jnforensics.com

http://www.statementanalysis.com

Other articles referred to in the book

Spanish unemployment article

http://www.dailymail.co.uk/news/article-2267619/Spanish-unemployment-leaps-new-high-26-55-young-people-work.html

Humintell eye contact myth article

http://www.humintell.com/2009/09/the-eye-contact-myth

Humintell coffee machine article

http://www.humintell.com/2013/09/sleepy-facial-expressions-deliver-free-coffee/

Baltimore Ravens fans are the most superstitious in the NFL

http://www.bizjournals.com/baltimore/news/2013/10/03/ravens-fans-superstitious-in-nfl.html

How are humans going to become extinct?

http://www.bbc.co.uk/news/business-22002530

Jeremy Hunt highlights the plight of the 'chronically lonely'.

http://www.bbc.co.uk/news/uk-politics-24572231

Liverpool teenagers sentenced for homeless man's murder

http://www.bbc.co.uk/news/uk-england-merseyside-22155807

Bibliography

Leeds jail full moon article

http://www.dailymail.co.uk/news/article-460050/Theres-violence-moons-say-police.html#ixzz2iGuC2Vo6

Daily Mail top 10 superstitions article

http://www.dailymail.co.uk/femail/article-2230328/Britons-superstitions-Walking-ladders-breaking-mirrors-opening-umbrellas-indoors.html

Binge drinking said to be tied to full moon

http://rense.com/health3/shine.htm

Crackdown on lunar-fuelled crime

http://news.bbc.co.uk/1/hi/england/southern_counties/6723911.stm

Auto accidents rise 14% during Full Moon, U.K. insurer says

http://www.bloomberg.com/apps/news?pid=newsarchive&sid=aFPQNod4LRn4

Study confirms myth of lunar cycle driving us mad is false... but doctors claim more mental health patients come in at full moon

http://www.dailymail.co.uk/news/article-2235964/Full-moon-Patient-study-confirms-common-myth-lunar-patterns-driving-mad-false.html

Golf superstitions

http://www.ncga.org/magazine/spring/brady.htm

Top 10 sporting superstitions

http://www.mirrorfootball.co.uk/news/Kolo-Toure-and-the-Top-10-sporting-superstitions-article28387.html

The Friday the 13th effect: why so many restaurants are missing a table 13

http://www.theguardian.com/lifeandstyle/2012/jul/11/restaurants-missing-table-13

The oddest airline superstitions

http://online.wsj.com/news/articles/SB10001424052702304176904579111350872569482

Connect With Me

I love connecting with people who share my passion, so please join me on Facebook and Twitter.

https://www.facebook.com/cjbaxx

https://twitter.com/bodylanguageuk

CPSIA information can be obtained at www.ICGtesting.com
Printed in the USA
LVOW12s1827260214

375256LV00001B/171/P